iOS 13 For Seniors

A RIDICULOUSLY SIMPLE GUIDE TO GETTING STARTED WITH THE LATEST IPHONE OPERATING SYSTEM

Scott La Counte

RIDICULOUSLY
SIMPLE BOOKS

ANAHEIM, CALIFORNIA

www.RidiculouslySimpleBooks.com

Table of Contents

Disclaimer: *Please note, while every effort has been made to ensure accuracy, this book is not endorsed by Apple, Inc. and should be considered unofficial.*

INTRODUCTION

The iPhone can be a little overwhelming. It seems to do everything! And that's part of the problem—you don't need to do everything. Of course you want to take stunning photos of the grandkids, but you probably can't think of a good reason you'd want to set up a private network or iMAP / POP email account.

You want the basics. How to take photos. How to Use Facetime with grandkids. And how to create custom Animoji's!

This book walks you through what you need to know step-by-step—including how navigation works now that the Home button is gone on newer iPhones.

It covers only what most people want to know—so you don't have to comb through hundreds of pages of tech-speak just to find out how to do a common feature.

The guide is based on new iPhone's that no longer have the Home button (iPhone X and up), so if you are updating from an earlier advice, then this guide won't be as useful to you.

This book is based on the book "The Ridiculously Simple Guide to iPhone 11, iPhone Pro, and iPhone Pro Max" but includes an expanded section on accessibility (like how to make text easier to see).

Are you ready to start enjoying your new iPhone? Then let's get started!

[1]

QUICK iOS OVERVIEW

This chapter will cover:
- The iPhones buttons
- What's Face ID
- What are the new features to iOS 13
- How to use the iPhone when it doesn't have a physical Home button

COMPATIBILITY

Good things don't last forever. Every year, Apple comes out with a new OS that's absolutely free—if your phone is compatible. The good news is that Apple supports its devices for several years; the bad news is they don't support devices forever. That means your beloved phone that just won't die might not be getting an upgrade. What's compatible?

- iPhone 11
- iPhone Pro and Pro Max
- iPhone XS and Max
- iPhone X and XR
- iPhone 8 and 8+
- iPhone 7 and 7+
- iPhone 6S and 6S+

- iPhone SE
- iPod Touch (seventh generation)

How to Get It

If you have auto updates on, then there's nothing you need to do. It will download on its own (usually while you sleep). If you want to do it manually, or see if auto updates are on, go to Settings > General > Software Updates.

The update is quite large, so make sure you download it over Wi-Fi and not data. Once it's downloaded, it will take several minutes to install and you won't be able to use your phone for some of this time, so make sure you aren't expecting any calls.

Phone Comparison

This year's slate of new iPhones introduced three new phones: iPhone 11, iPhone Pro, and iPhone Pro Max.

Aside from size and price, it can be difficult to understand the difference. If you haven't purchased a phone yet, this section will break down what the difference is.

The first thing I'll point out is the iPhone Pro and iPhone Pro Max are essentially the same phone with two distinctions: size (both weight and dimensions) and battery life (the Max will last about an hour longer than the normal pro).

Size and Build

One of the things that really stood out with the 2018 models was the top notch. What I mean by that is there was a small area on the top of the screen that was cut out for the camera. You get used to it, but it's still a little annoying when you're watching a movie and there's a small portion of the screen gone. On this year's Pro models, the notch is gone; on the iPhone 11, the notch is still there.

Screen-wise, the specs are pretty straight forward: the Pro Max is the largest (6.5 inches); the Pro and iPhone 11 are almost the same (5.8 inches on the Pro and 6.1 inches on the 11). While the size is pretty close to the same, the Pro models have a higher definition: 458 ppi vs. 326 ppi.

The Pro models are also slightly more water resistant: 4mm vs. 2mm.

The Pros are built with a textured matte glass and stainless-steel design; the iPhone 11 has a glass and aluminum design. What does that mean? The Pro is built to be more durable and more scratch resistant.

Battery

If battery is important to you, then the Max is the best you can get (20 hours playing video vs. 18 hours of playing video on regular Pro and 17 hours on the iPhone 11).

The Pro models also ship with a 18w adaptor for faster charging. These adaptors are USB-C and the cable you get is USB-C to lightning (not regular USB to lightning). USB-C is becoming the standard for charging and will most likely replace the lightning adaptor in due time.

Camera

If you buy a phone for the camera and want the very best, then you'll find that on the Pro models. The Pro models have three cameras; the iPhone 11 has two. What's up with the extra camera? That's for tel-ephoto. The Pro models also have what many critics are calling the "camera bump"; that means the lens on the Pro sticks out a little more. It may not look pretty, but what I would keep in mind is you will most likely have a case on it and it won't be that noticeable. It's the tradeoff for having a superior camera.

What phone is right for you? It all comes down to preference. All of the phones are powerful with cameras that will deliver impressive re-sults. The Pros are several hundred dollars more. They are built better, but what you have to ask yourself is if that is worth the price. The iPh-one 11 is fast, has a great battery, and takes photos that are better than most phones.

[2]

WHAT HAPPENED TO THE HOME BUTTON?

This chapter will cover:
- The iPhones buttons
- What's Face ID
- What are the new features to iOS 13
- How to use the iPhone when it doesn't have a physical Home button

TAKE ME HOME

Chances are you've had an iPhone or, at the very least, used an iPhone. You know all about that button on the bottom of the phone—that glorious round thing with a square in the middle that always takes you home. It's amazing. Or it was! Because it's gone!

So, the real elephant in the room with the iPhone X and up is the Home button, or lack thereof. In the next chapter, I'll talk about getting set up, so I know this all sounds a little backwards, but because a lot of people are upgrading to the new iPhone from an earlier model, it's worth talking about the main things that will be different.

If you have used the iPhone before, then I bet you'll spend a good day continuously putting your thumb where the button used to be!

Don't worry! You're going to get through it. In fact, after you get used to it not being there, you'll actually start seeing it's more effective without it.

Before diving into the gestures, let's cover some other things that look different about this phone.

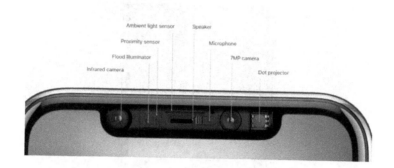

The top portion of the phone (it's known as the top notch) is a black strip. All of it helps your phone work better. To the far right (looking at the phone) is a Dot Projector. It sounds like something that will project your iPhone onto the wall, doesn't it? I wish! That's actually the camera that scans your face for Face ID (I'll cover that in just a second). Next to that is the camera; it's 12MP. There are a few other sensors and cameras to the far left. They all sound fancy, don't they? Proximity sensor. Flood illuminator. Fancy is...well fancy! But what on Earth does that mean in simple terms? It means that the front-facing camera can take pretty impressive selfies! If you've used the iPhone 8 or 8 Plus then you're probably familiar with Portrait mode? If not, in a nutshell, it gives a blurred, professional look to your photo. To do that, you need some extra sensors; beginning with the iPhone X (and any iPhone after), those features are on both the front and back of the phone. That means you can get the same type of photos no matter which camera you use (front or back).

Okay, so all that's interesting, right? But you don't actually do anything with the notch. What about the buttons on the phone itself? Good question! Thanks for asking!

The button placement isn't too far off from previous iPhones.

On the right side of the phone, you have your volume up and down, which does what? You guessed it! Turns your volume up and down! There's also a switch above it that will silence sound.

On the left side you have your "Side Button." Legend has it, they named it the Side Button because it's on the side of the phone! That button is on other phones—albeit a tad shorter—but it functions a little bit differently here.

The Side Button is and isn't the Home button replacement. That sounds vague, huh? Here's what I mean: you won't use this button to get back to the Home screen, but you can use it to activate Siri (or you can just say "Hey Siri"). You also use this button to power the phone on and off—or to put it in standby (which is the mode you put it in after you finish playing Angry Birds in the bathroom and need to set the phone down for a minute to wash your hands).

The most common use for the Side Button is to wake up your phone. Picking up your phone and staring at it with an annoyed or confused expression will also do this. But if you ever find yourself stuck and picking up the phone isn't waking it up, then just push down on the Side Button and you should be just fine.

That Side Button is also going to come in handy when you want to use Apple Pay—double push the button and then stare at your phone sadly as money is magically taken away.

FACE ID

Things were going okay with you and the Home button. You could rub your thumb over it and like a genie in a bottle, it would magically read your DNA and turn on. Why'd Apple have to go and ruin a good thing?

Sure, getting rid of the button gives you more screen real estate, but plenty of other phones have added a button to the back of the phone so you can have the best of both worlds. It's like Apple is trying to force you to love it, isn't it? I don't know why Apple does everything, but if past history teaches us anything, we have learned that Apple makes us adapt to better things by taking away the things we love. We loved our CD drives...and Apple took them out and put USB drives in their place; we got through it, though didn't we?! They did it again with the headphone jack. And on new MacBook's, USB is gone and in its place, the faster USB-C.

Change is never fun, but it's not necessarily a bad thing. If you like numbers, you'll love this one. That little finger scanner on your old phone has a ratio of 50,000:1—that's the ratio of how hard it would be for someone to break into your phone. The iPhone with Face ID? 1,000,000:1. So if you're a fan of security, then Face ID is a no-brainer.

If you're that person who is always throwing "What if" into the equation (you're the same person who morbidly asked, "What if someone stole my phone and cut off my finger to unlock it? Would the fingerprint scanner still work?"), then I'm sure you have a few questions. Like:

- What if I wear glasses and then take them off or put in contacts?
- What if I have a beard and shave it?
- What if I think I look like Brad Pitt, but the phone says I'm more of a Lyle Lovett?

Sorry, Lyle, not everyone can be a Brad—but you don't have to worry about those first two points. Face ID has adaptive recognition, so you'll be just fine if you decide to grow it out for Movember.

If you're in a dark room, Face ID will also still work—albeit with a little bit of help from the light sensor—which is a little annoying if you're lying in bed and the only way to unlock your phone is to have a light turn on to scan your face. If you're in a dark room, you can also just press that Side Button to open it manually and skip Face ID.

FEATURE THIS...

Every year, Apple releases a new version of its popular iPhone operating system that includes lots of changes. This year is no different. The update is completely free (if your phone is compatible).

While some of the features are pretty obvious, others are more under the hood and you may not be aware of them. Some updates are also exclusive to new devices.

This section will cover some of the most popular things that are new or updated in iOS 13. Most of them will be covered in greater detail as you continue through the book.

Performance

Changes behind the scenes means that phones now run faster and smoother; if your phone has Face ID, it will unlock up to 30% faster.

Dark Mode

Dark mode is perhaps the most obvious change to iOS; it lets you change your background to black, which makes the phone easier to read in dark or nighttime settings.

Look Around

You may have noticed a weird looking car with a giant camera on top driving around your neighborhood. For years, these cars were operated by Google, but over the past several months, Apple has been quietly working on its own street view-ish service called Look Around.

The new feature launches in iOS 13. Not all cities will be available at launch.

Find My

Finding your devices has been available for a long time on iOS; iOS 13 takes it up a notch, however, by letting you find devices even when Wi-Fi and cellular are turned off. This is accomplished by using the Bluetooth radios of other nearby devices.

Photos and Videos

Photos and videos will be covered more extensively later; what's changed, however, is how they are organized and the editing features available. In short, finding the best photo is easier and editing is more powerful.

Reminders

The Reminder app has a new user interface (UI) and is now easier to share lists with friends and family.

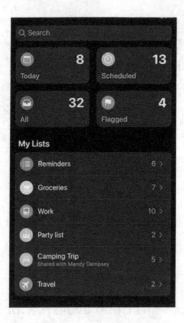

Memoji & Animoji

Memojis have even more customizations. Animoji has more characters.

Notes

Notes has added a gallery view and you can now share entire folders.

Mail

Mail has made it easier to block and mute people, but the biggest change is with formatting your emails.

Files

You can now use an SD Card or USB cable on your device in a way that's more like a computer when viewing and opening files (not just importing photos).

QuickPath Keyboard

If you don't like the traditional keyboard and prefer to swipe to keys (it's faster once you get used to it), iOS 13 has introduced a new keyboard that does just that.

Wireless Controllers

Apple has invested a lot in one of their newest services: Apple Arcade. To enhance it, they have added support for popular wireless game controllers (notably PlayStation DualShock 4 controller and the Xbox One S controller).

Read Goals

iBooks had added goals so you can now be encouraged to read more.

Screenshots

The ability to take a screenshots has been on the iPhone for years; iOS 13, however, introduces the option to take a screenshot of the entire page as a PDF.

Optimized Battery Charging

Your phone battery starts slowly deteriorating from the moment you turn it on. Much of this is because of overcharging. iOS 13 works harder to get the most out of your battery. It learns your charging routine, and then will start charging it only to 80%, and then charge the remaining just before you unplug it. So, it will not be charging for the entire night.

There are obviously more updates to iOS; some are too minor to cover and some will be covered later in this book.

If you want the big giant list of everything new in iOS 13, visit: https://www.apple.com/ios/ios-13/features/

THANKS FOR THE NICE GESTURE, APPLE!

And now the moment you've been reading for: how to make your way around a phone without the Home button.

Let's Go Home

First, the easiest gesture: getting to your Home screen. Do you have your pen and paper ready? It's complicated...swipe up from the bottom of your screen.

That's it.

It's not too far off from pushing a button. Heck, your finger's even in the same place! The only difference is you're moving your thumb upward instead of inward.

Multitask

As Dorothy would say, there's no place like Home—but we can still give a shoutout to Multitask can't we? If you don't know what it is, Multitask is how you switch quickly between apps—you're in iMessage and want to open up Safari to get a website, for example; instead of closing iMessage, finding Safari from the Home screen, and then repeating the process to get back, you use Multitask to do it quickly.

On the old iPhones you would double press the Home button. On the new iPhone, you swipe up from the bottom as if you were going to Home...but don't lift your finger; instead of lifting your finger, continue swiping up until you reach the middle of your screen—at this point, you should see the Multitask interface.

If you have an app open (Note: this does not work on the Home screen), you can also slide your finger right across the bottom edge of the screen; this will go to the previous app open.

Mission Control...We're Go for Flashlight
If you haven't noticed, I'm putting these features in order of use. So, the third most common gesture people use is the Control Center.

That's where all your controls are located—go figure...Control is where controls are!

We'll go over the Control Center in more detail later in the book. For now, just know that this is where you'll do things like adjust brightness, enable airplane mode, and turn on the beloved flashlight. On the old iPhone, you accessed Control Center by swiping up from the bottom of the screen. No Bueno on the new iPhone—if you recall, swiping up gets you Home.

The new gesture for Control Center is swiping down from the upper right corner of the iPhone (not the top middle, which will do something else).

Notify Me How to Get Notifications

Eck! So many gestures to remember! Let me throw you a bone. To see notifications (those are the alerts like email and text that you get on your phone), swipe down from the middle of the screen. That's the same way you did it before! Finally, nothing new to remember!

I hate to steal your bone back, but about not remembering anything new: there is something to remember. :-(

As you recall, if you swipe down from the right corner you get the Control Center; that wasn't the case on old phones. Swiping down anywhere on top got you to the Notifications screen. On the X and up, you can only swipe in the top-middle for notifications.

Searching for Answers

If you're like me, you probably have a million apps—and because you want to see the wallpaper on your phone's Home screen, you put those million apps in one folder! That may not be the best way to organize a library, but the search function on the iPhone, makes it easy to find anything quickly.

In addition to apps, you can use search to find calendar dates, contacts, things on the Internet. The best part of search? Works the same way it does on older iPhones...there's your bone back! From your Home screen, swipe down in the middle of the screen.

Calling All Widgets

Many apps come with what's known as a widget. Widgets are basically mini versions of your favorite app—so you can see the weather, for example, without actually opening the app.

The gesture to see widgets is the same on the new phone as the old. Hurray! Something else you don't have to learn. From the Home or Lock screen, swipe right and they'll come out.

Reach for the Sky

Several years ago, Apple made a big change to the iPhone by making things...well big! They introduced what would be known as the "plus" model. It was wonderful...and big! If you had Shaq hands, then you'd have no problem getting around the device. If you had normal human hands, then the apps on the top row of the phone were a bit of a stretch.

This wasn't a huge problem on the iPhone X because it was a little smaller than the plus. The next generation phones, however, introduced a "max" model. On the old phones, this was a snap—just double tap (not press, tap) the Home button. New phones? Sorry, but we're back to learning new things...I'm all out of bones for this chapter.

To reach the top, swipe down on the bottom edge of the screen.

FORCE RESTARTING

Ideally you should never have to force reset your phone (that means your phone is frozen and you can't do anything). If it ever happens, then what do you do with no Home button?! Not to fret! It's pretty simple:

1. Quickly press and release the Volume Up button.
2. Quickly press and release the Volume Down button.
3. Press and hold the Side button until you see the apple Logo.

Those are the options for forcing your phone to shut off. What if it's not frozen and you just want to turn it off? Press and hold the Side button and Volume Up at the same time. This brings up several options—Slide to power off, Medical ID, and Emergency SOS. The one you want is obviously the first. SOS will call local emergency services, so don't slide that by mistake!

THE RIDICULOUSLY SIMPLE CHAPTER ONE RECAP

Okay, so you only got a minute to get up and running, and you need the 1-minute summary of everything important?

Let's cover gestures. The left side will be the way the gesture used to work, and right side will be the way it works on new iPhones.

iPhone 8 and Down	iPhone X and Up
Go to the Home screen - Press the Home button.	Go to the Home screen - Swipe up from the bottom of your screen.
Multitask - Double press Home button.	Multitask - Swipe up from the bottom of your screen, but don't lift your finger until it reaches the middle of the screen.
Control Center - Swipe up from the bottom of the screen.	Control Center - Swipe down from the upper right corner of the screen.
Notifications - Swipe down from the top of the screen.	Notifications - Swipe down from the middle top of the screen.
Search - From the Home screen, swipe down from the middle of your screen.	Search - From the Home screen, swipe down from the middle of your screen.
Access Widgets - From the Home or Lock screen, swipe right.	Access Widgets - From the Home or Lock screen, swipe right.
Reach the Top - Double tap (not press) the Home button.	Reach the Top - Swipe down on the bottom edge of the screen.

[3]

HELLO, WORLD

This chapter will cover:
- Setting up your iPhone for the first time
- Setting up your iPhone with your previous phone's settings
- Setting up Face ID
- Charging
- Navigating around the phone using gestures, 3D touch and more
- Using the on-screen keyboard

SETTING THINGS UP

Now that you know about the main differences between the physical nature of the phone, let's take a step back and talk about setting it up. If you're already at the Home screen, you can obviously skip this section.

Unboxing the iPhone shouldn't throw you any surprises. It doesn't have a manual, but that's normal for Apple. You can find the manual on Apple's website (https://support.apple.com/manuals/iphone) if that's something you'd like to see. What is worth pointing out is the headphones. A few years back, Apple decided for us that we no longer needed a normal headphone jack. How sweet, right? But to be nice, they always threw in a 3.5m Lightning Adapter—so you could use any headphones when it was plugged in. New models ditch that. If you're keen on using it, then you can buy one for under $10.

Once you turn the phone on with the Side Button, it will load to a setup screen. Setup can be intimating to a lot of people, but Apple's setup is probably the easiest one you'll ever do—even my mom, who hates all electronics, had no problem doing it on her own.

It's pretty straightforward. I suppose I could just write everything that you'll see on the screen, but it seems a little redundant since you are seeing it on the screen. In a nutshell, it's going to ask you your pre-ferred language and country, your wireless network (make sure you connect to your wireless network here, or it's going to start download-ing a lot of apps over your LTE, which will eat up your data), and you'll need to activate your device with your wireless carrier.

So that's the basics. There are a few options after here that might be a little less straightforward. The first is a question that asks if you want Location Services turned on. I recommend saying yes. This is how the Map will automatically know where you are. Or when you take a photo at Boring Town, USA, and several years later you say "Where on Earth was this photo taken?" you'll know exactly where it was taken if Location Services is turned on. Remember: anything you don't turn on here (or that you do turn on) can be changed later. So, if you change your mind, it's fine.

You Should Know: Anytime Location Services is being used in an app, you will see a small arrow icon in the upper right corner of your screen.

FACE ID

Face ID is probably one of the features you hear about the most. It lets your phone scan your face to unlock it—it's more secure than your fingerprint. To get started, just tap the Get Started button.

Next, you'll be directed to put your face in the center of the camera; then you basically move your head around, so the camera can see all of your features. It's kind of like rolling your neck around. It takes about 20 seconds to complete.

Once it's done, you'll get a message. That's it. Your phone is now ready to unlock at the sight of your gorgeous face!

After you set up Face ID, you'll be prompted to enter a passcode. Why do you need a passcode when you have a Face ID? The biggest reason is there may be times when you don't want to use Face ID: like if it's dark and you don't want a bunch of light illuminated from your phone, or you have a friend who needs to get into your phone.

By default, the passcode is six digits. If you don't want to add one, tap "Don't Add Passcode"; in this same area, you can also change it to a four-digit passcode. My only advice here is to be creative: don't use the same four digits as your bank pin, or the last four of your social. And remember: you can change it later.

Once security options are set up, you'll have the option to restore from a backup. If you have a previous iPhone, I would recommend doing this—it will save you time adjusting some of the settings later.

If you have decided to restore from a backup, then make sure your backup is up-to-date. On your old iPhone, go to Settings, then tap your name on the top (it will probably have a picture of you), next tap "iCloud," and finally go to "iCloud Backup." It might be set to automatic. However, just to make sure you get everything, I would tap "Back Up Now." Below the Back Up Now option, you can see when the last backup was performed.

You're almost done! But first Apple needs to understand how to take your money! The next screen is creating an Apple ID. If you already have one, then sign in; if you don't have one, then create a free one. Don't want to give Apple your hard-earned money? I don't blame you! They did, after all, just take $1,000+ from you for your phone! But you still need an Apple ID. Don't worry—you don't have to give them any more money if you really don't want to, but I'm sure you'll want to download free apps (like Facebook), and you'll need an Apple ID for that as well.

Once your phone is all done thinking about how it will take your money, it will be time to set up iCloud. Again, this is something I recommend setting up. iCloud backs everything up remotely; so, if you want to share things across multiple devices (your Apple Watch, iPad, MacBook, Apple TV, for example) it's a breeze.

After iCloud is Apple Pay. "Wait," you say! "I thought Apple already asked how they were going to get more money?!" They did! This is all about how others will take your money! Once you have an expensive phone, everyone wants a piece of you! Apple Pay will basically create a virtual credit card so when you're at the grocery store you can pay by tapping your phone instead of whipping out your wallet.

Apple also has a card of its own (Apple Card) that I'll cover later.

Is Apple Pay really safe? In a word: yes. It's safer than the card you carry around in your wallet. Unlike that card, no one can see the numbers on it. And if someone were to steal your phone, they wouldn't be able to use Apple Pay unless they knew your password. The encryption on Apple Pay is also much more sophisticated—you are much more likely to get your number hacked online than on your phone.

Most banks are on Apple Pay, but unfortunately some are not. If you don't see yours, you will have to wait. You can't add it manually.

Next up is iCloud Keychain. Like most things in the setup, it's all about what you are comfortable with. Keychain stores all your passwords in one place. So, if you are shopping online, you don't have to add it in or remember it. It's all secure—no one can see it but you. And, of course, you can turn it on or off later.

Only a few more steps! Painless so far, right?

Up next is Siri. Siri is your personal assistant. You can say things like, "Hey, Siri: what's the weather?" and like magic, she'll tell you. I'll cover it later in the book, but for now I would turn it on.

After enabling Siri, decide whether or not to report diagnostic and usage data to Apple. If you're worried about privacy, tap "About Diagnostics and Privacy" to learn what information Apple will receive and how it will be used.

Finally, decide whether or not you'd like to use a zoomed-in display or not. If you prefer larger icons, you can choose Zoomed View for a magnified display. It's entirely up to you, and this setting can be changed later.

And finally, setup is done! The last screen says "Welcome to iPh-one - Get Started." Tapping on that will bring you to the Home screen, and that's where the fun really starts.

Welcome to iPhone

Get Started

I FEEL CHARGED!

Before digging into using your phone deeper, I want to talk really quickly about charging. You probably know how to plug the charger into your phone. If you can't figure out how to stick an out-y into an in-y, then call that nephew who never returns your phone call and ask him. He's going to love hearing from you, I'm sure.

What might not be so obvious is the iPhone doesn't need to be plugged into anything to be charged. New iPhones can be charged wirelessly. To do this you need what's called a "Qi charger." They're not terribly expensive ($20 range). Qi chargers are compatible with other phones, so a lot of cafes and hotels have them ready to use. To use it, you just set your phone on top of the wireless charging mat and make sure the charging light (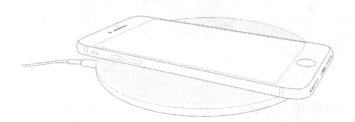) comes on. It's really simple.

If you have the iPhone Pro or Pro Max, then the charger does look a little bit different. That's because it includes a USB-C adapter for faster charging. You can still use a lightening adapter / USB, but it's going to take longer.

ENOUGH ABOUT SETUP! HOW DO I USE THIS THING, ALREADY?!

The iPhone is a touchscreen device, so to use it you'd think you'd have to worry about only one thing: touching it!

That's true. But there are different ways you can touch it. Fortunately, unlike gestures (mentioned in Chapter One), nothing has really changed; so, if you know how to use gestures, you'll be just fine. Below is a quick summary:

Tap

This is the "click" of the iPhone world. A tap is just a brief touch. It doesn't have to be hard or last very long. You'll tap icons, hyperlinks, form choices, and more. You'll also tap numbers on a touch keypad in order to make calls. It's not exactly rocket science, is it?

Tap and Hold

This simply means touching the screen and leaving your finger in contact with the glass. It's useful for bringing up context menus or other options in some apps.

Double Tap

This refers to two rapid taps, like double clicking with your finger. Double tapping will perform different functions in different apps. It will also zoom in on pictures or webpages.

Swipe

Swiping means putting your finger on the surface of your screen and dragging it to a certain point and then removing your finger from the surface. You'll use this motion to navigate through menu levels in your apps, through pages in Safari, and more. It'll become second nature overnight, I promise.

Drag

This is mechanically the same as swiping, but with a different purpose. You'll touch an object to select it, and then drag it to wherever it needs to go and release it. It's just like dragging and dropping with a mouse, but it skips the middleman.

Pinch

Take two fingers, place them on the iPhone screen, and move them either toward each other or away from each other in a pinching or reverse pinching motion. Moving your fingers together will zoom in inside many apps, including web browsers and photo viewers; moving them apart will zoom out.

Rotate and Tilt

Many apps on iPhone take advantage of rotating and tilting the device itself. For instance, in the paid app Star Walk, you can tilt the screen so that it's pointed at whatever section of the night sky you're interested in—Star Walk will reveal the constellations based on the direction the iPhone is pointed.

How Do You Send Cute Emojis to Everyone?

The reason you got an iPhone is to send adorable emojis with your text messages, obviously! So how do you do it? It's all in the keyboard, so I'll cover that next!

Anytime you type a message, the keyboard pops up automatically. There are no extra steps. But there are a few things you can do with the keyboard to make it more personal.

There are a few things to notice on the keyboard—the delete key is marked with a little 'x' (it's right next to the letter M), and the shift key is the key with the upward arrow (next to the letter Z).

By default, the first letter you type will be capitalized. You can tell what case the letters are in though at a quick glance.

To use the shift key, just tap it and then tap the letter you want to capitalize or the alternate punctuation you'd like to use. Alternatively, you can touch the shift key and drag your finger to the letter you want to capitalize. Double tap the shift key to enter caps lock (i.e. everything is capitalized) and tap once to exit caps lock.

Special Characters

To type special characters, just press and hold the key of the associated letter until options pop up. Drag your finger to the character you want to use and be on your way. What exactly would you use this for? Let's say you're are writing something in Spanish and need the accent on the "e"; tapping and holding on the "e" will bring that option up.

Using Dictation

Let's face it: typing on the keyboard stinks sometimes! Wouldn't it be easier to just say what you want to write? If that sounds like you, then Dictation can help! Just tap the microphone next to the spacebar and start talking. It works pretty well.

Number and Symbol Keyboards

Of course, there's more to life than letters and exclamation points. If you need to use numbers, tap the 123 key in the bottom left corner. This will bring up a different keyboard with numbers and punctuation.

From this keyboard, you can get back to the alphabet by tapping the ABC key in the bottom left corner. You can also access an additional keyboard which includes the remaining standard symbols by tapping the #+- key, just above the ABC key.

Emoji Keyboard

And finally, the moment you've waited for! Emojis!

The emoji keyboard is accessible using the smiley face key between the 123 key and the dictation key. Emojis are tiny cartoon images that you can use to liven up your text messages or other written output. This goes far beyond the colon-based emoticons of yesteryear—there are enough emojis on your iPhone to create an entire visual vocabulary.

To use the emoji keyboard, note that there are categories along the bottom (and that the globe icon on the far left will return you to the world of language). Within those categories, there are several screens of pictographs to choose from. Many of the human emojis include multicultural variations. Just press and hold them to reveal other options.

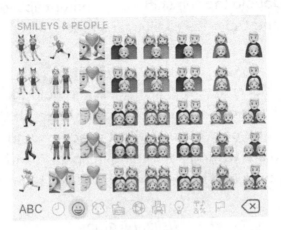

Multilingual Typing

Most people are probably all set. They know all they need to know about typing on the iPhone and they're ready to blast emojis at their friends. There are a few other features that apply to some (not all people).

One such feature is Multilingual Typing. This is for people who type multiple languages at the same time. So, if you type between Spanish and English, you won't keep seeing a message saying your spelling is wrong.

If that sounds like you, then you just need to enable another dictionary, which is simple. Go to Settings > General > Dictionary.

Configuring International Keyboards

If you find yourself typing in a different language fairly often, you may want to set up international keyboards. To set up international keyboards, visit Settings > General > Keyboard > Keyboards. You can then add an appropriate international keyboard by tapping "Add New Keyboard." As an example, iPhone has great support for Chinese text entry—choose from pinyin, stroke, zhuyin, and handwriting, where you actually sketch out the character yourself.

When you enable another keyboard, the smiley face key will change to a globe icon. To use international keyboards, tap the globe key to cycle through your keyboard choices.

Your iPhone is loaded with features to help prevent slip-ups, including Apple's battle-tested autocorrect feature which guards against common typos. In iOS 8, Apple introduced a predictive text feature that predicts what words you're most likely to type, and its accuracy is even better in the new iOS.

Three choices appear just above the keyboard—the entry as typed, plus two best guesses. Predictive text is somewhat context-specific, too. It learns your speech patterns as you email your boss or text your best friend, and it will serve up appropriate suggestions based on who you're messaging or emailing. Of course if it bothers you, you can visit Settings > General > Keyboards and turn off predictive text by sliding the green slider to the left.

Third Party Keyboards

Lastly, you can add third-party keyboards to your phone. So, if you hate the iPhone keyboard and want something similar to what's on Android, then you can go to the App Store and get it (more on that later).

[4]

THE BASICS

This chapter will cover:
- Home screen
- Making calls
- Adding and removing apps
- Sending messages
- iMessage apps
- Notifications
- AirDrop

WELCOME HOME

There's one thing that has pretty much stayed the same since the very first iPhone was released: the Home screen. The look has evolved, but the layout has not. All you need to know about it is it's the main screen. So, when you read "go to the Home screen," this is the screen I'm talking about. Make sense?

CONTROL CENTER

Even if you don't know the term for it, you probably have used Control Center; it's where you'll find shortcuts that control commonly used features on your phone, like volume and the camera.

Control Center is more powerful than it used to be. iOS 13 introduced two new features to the Control Center: Night Mode and joining Wi-Fi network (covered below). However, there are older features you might not be aware of.

Swipe in the upper right corner to bring down your Control Center.

Using Control Center

Let's take a look around each section of Control Center. The first group is what controls the wireless activity on your phone. Starting in the upper left corner, the airplane icon is Airplane Mode, which quickly turns off all cellular, Wi-Fi, and Bluetooth; next to that is the Cellular Data; under the airplane is the Wi-Fi toggle; and finally, the Bluetooth toggle.

If you long-press any of these buttons, then you'll get an expanded list of options.

If you long-press the Wi-Fi button on the above screen, then you get all the Wi-Fi networks within range, and you can join one—you no longer have to go into your Settings app to join a Wi-Fi network.

Under the wireless settings is: screen rotation lock (press it and your screen won't autorotate when you tilt your phone sideways), Do Not Disturb mode, and Screen Mirroring (if you have an Apple TV, you use this button to mirror your phone to your TV).

Over on the right side is the Music control (tap in the upper right corner of that and you can select where you want to listen to music if you have an AirPlay device—such as AirPods or HomePod). Below that is the phone brightness and volume.

Long-press the brightness button and you can select if you want night mode turned on. Night mode turns areas of your phone that are white to black—for example when you are reading a book in iBooks, the pages are dark. You can also use Night Shift here, which lessens the amount of blue light that emits from your phone—exposure to this kind of light at night can affect your sleeping habits.

At the bottom of Control Center is the Flashlight, Timer, Calculator, Camera Shortcut, Screen Record (I'll cover why you may not have this below), and Apple TV remote (again, you may or may not have this).

Long-pressing most of these will bring up shortcuts to options for the app. Long- pressing the camera button, for example, will bring up shortcuts to different kinds of photos you can take.

Customizing Control Center

You can add and remove some of the options on the Control Panel by going to **Settings > Control Center**, then selecting Customize Controls.

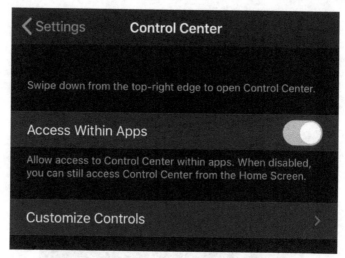

The top has the controls currently included (the ones you can re-move, that is). Hit the red minus to remove them.

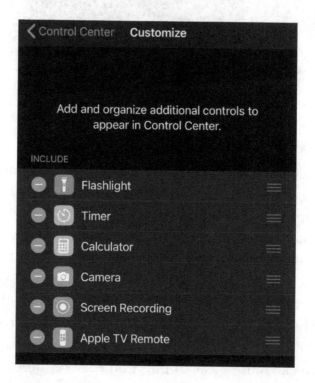

Remember I said there were some controls I had that you may not? Here's where you can add them in. Below this are the ones that you can add to Control Center. Tap the plus sign to add them.

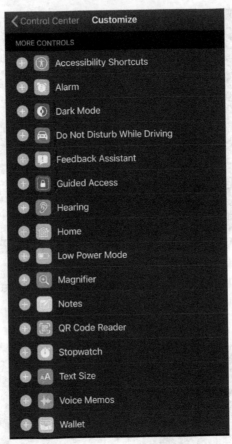

Making Calls

You know what always amazes me when I see commercials for the iPhone? It's a phone, but people never seem to be talking on it! But it actually can make phone calls!

If you actually need to call someone, then tap the green Phone icon in the lower left corner of your Home screen. This will bring up the iPhone's keypad. Tap in your number and hit the green Call button. To hang up, just tap the red End button at the bottom of the screen. You'll see other options on the call screen, too. If you needed to use the keypad while on a call, just tap the Keypad circle to bring it up. Similarly, you can mute a call or put it on speaker here.

Receiving a call is fairly intuitive. When your phone rings, your iPhone will tell you who's calling. If their name is stored in your contacts (more on this later), it'll be displayed. All you have to do is swipe to answer the call. There are some additional options as well—you can ask iPhone to remind you of the call later by tapping "Remind Me," or you can respond with a text message. iOS 13 includes some handy canned responses, including "Can't talk right now…", "I'll call you later," "I'm on my way," and "What's up?" You can also send a custom message if you need to. If you miss a call, iPhone will let you know the next time you wake up your phone. By default, you can respond to a missed call directly from the Lock screen.

When a call from an unknown number comes in, iPhone will check other apps like Mail where phone numbers might be found. Using that information, it will make a guess for you and let you know who might be calling. Kind of creepy, right? But also really useful.

If you want to feel extra special, you can have Siri announce your call. To turn this feature on, go to Settings > Phone > Announce Calls. Select Always, Headphones & Car, Headphones Only or Never to choose your preferred way to announce calls.

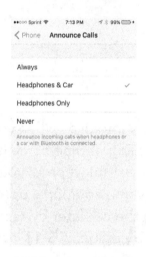

THERE'S AN APP FOR THAT

App is short for application. So, when you hear the term "There's an app for that," it just means there's a program that does what you want to do. If you're a Windows user, all those things you always open (like Word and Excel) are apps. Apple has literally millions of apps. Opening an app is as simple as touching it.

Unlike apps on a computer, you don't have to close apps on your phone. It's all automatic. For most apps, it will even remember where you were, so when you open it again it's saved.

ORGANIZING APPS

If you're like me—and pretty much most people are—you love your apps and you have a lot of them! So, you'll need to know how to move them around, put them in folders, and delete them. It's all easy to do.

The Home screen may be the first screen you see, but if you swipe to the right, you'll see there are more; you can have 11. Personally, I keep the most used apps on the first screen, and not-so-used apps in folders on the second. The bottom dock is where I put the apps that I use all the time (like Mail and Safari).

To rearrange apps, take your finger and touch one of your apps. Instead of tapping, hold your finger down for a few seconds; you'll see an app option pop up but keep holding until the apps jiggle. When the apps are jiggling like that, you can touch them without opening them and drag them around your screen. Try it out! Just touch an app and drag your finger to move it. When you've found the perfect spot, lift your finger and the app drops into place. After you've downloaded more apps, you can also drag apps across Home screens.

You can delete an app using the same method for moving them. The only difference is instead of moving them, you tap the 'x' in the upper left corner of the icon. Don't worry about deleting something on accident. Apps are stored in the cloud. You can delete and install them as many times as you want; you don't have to pay again—you just have to download them again.

Putting apps on different screens is helpful, but to be really organized you want to use folders. You can, for example, have a folder for all your game apps, finance apps, social apps, whatever you want. You pick what to name it. If you want an "Apps I use on the toilet" folder, then you can absolutely have it!

To create a folder, just drag one app over another app you'd like to add into that folder.

Once they are together, you can name the folder. To delete the folder, just put the folder apps in "jiggle mode" and drag them out of the folder. iPhone doesn't allow empty folders—when a folder is empty, iPhone deletes it automatically.

When you are finished organizing apps, tap the Done button in the upper right corner.

MESSAGING

More and more smartphone users are staying connected through text messages instead of phone calls, and the iPhone makes it easy to keep in touch with everyone. In addition to sending regular SMS text messages and multimedia messages (pictures, links, video clips and voice notes), you can also use iMessage to interact with other Apple users. This feature allows you to send instant messages to anyone signed into a Mac running OS X Mountain Lion or higher, or any iOS device running iOS 5 or greater. iMessage for iOS 13 has been completely changed to make everything just a little more...animated.

On the main Messages screen, you will be able to see the many different conversations you have going on. You can also delete conversations by swiping from right to left on the conversation you'd like and tapping the red Delete button. New conversations or existing conversations with new messages will be highlighted with a big blue dot next to it, and the Messages icon will have a badge displaying the number of unread messages you have, similar to the Mail and Phone icons.

To create a message, click on the Messages icon, then the Compose button in the top right corner.

Once the new message dialog box pops up, click on the plus button (+) to choose from your contacts list, or just type in the phone number of the person you wish to text. For group messages, just keep adding as many people as you'd like. Finally, click on the bottom field to begin typing your message.

iMessage has added in a lot of new features over the past few years. If all you want to do is send a message, then just tap the blue up arrow.

But you can do so much more than just send a message! (Please note, if you are sending a message with newer features to someone with an older OS or a non-Apple device, then it won't look as it appears on your screen).

To start with, go ahead and push (but don't release that blue button—or if you are using a phone with 3D Touch or Haptic touch, press down a little firmer). This will bring up several different animations for the message.

On the top of this screen, you'll also notice two tabs; one says "Bubble" and the other says "Screen"; if you tap "Screen" you can add animations to the entire screen. Swipe right and left to see each new animation.

When you get a message that you like and you want to respond to it, you can tap and hold your finger over the message or image; this will bring up different ways you can react.

Once you make your choice, the person on the receiving end will see how you responded.

If you'd like to add animation, a photo, a video, or lots of other things, then let's look at the options next to the message.

You have three choices—which bring up even more choices! The first is the camera, which lets you send photos with your message (or take new photos—note, these photos won't be saved on your phone), the next lets you use iMessage apps (more on that in a second), and the last lets you record a message with your voice.

Let's look at the camera option first.

If you just want to attach a photo to your message, then after you tap the camera, go to the upper left corner and tap the Photo icon; this brings up all the photos you can attach.

If you want to take an original photo, then tap the round button on the bottom. To add effects, tap the star in the lower left corner.

Tapping effects brings up all the different effects available to you. I'll talk more about Animoji soon, but as an example, this app lets you put an Animoji over your face (see the example below—not bad for an author photo, eh?!)

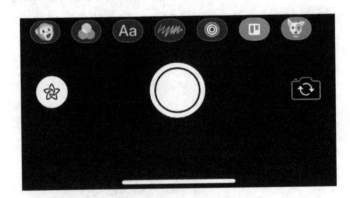

Finally, the last option is apps. You should know all about phone apps by now, but now there's a new set of apps called iMessage apps. These apps let you be both silly (send digital stickers) and serious (send cash to someone via text). To get started, tap the '+' button to open the iMessage App Store.

You can browse all the apps just like you would the regular App Store. Installing them is the same as well.

When you're ready to use the app, just tap apps, tap the app you want to load, and tap what you want to send. You can also drag stickers on top of messages. Just tap, hold and drag.

Also in the app section is a button called "#images."

If you tap on this button you can search for thousands of humorous memes and animated GIFs. Just tap it and search a term you want to find—such as "Money" or "Fight".

One final iMessage feature worth trying out is the personal handwritten note. Tap on a new message like you are going to start typing a new message; now rotate your phone horizontally. This brings up an option to use your finger to create a handwritten note. Sign away, and then hit done when you're finished.

NOTIFICATIONS

When you have your phone locked, you'll start seeing notifications at some point; this tells you things like "You have a new email," "Don't forget to set your alarm," etc.

So, when you see all your notifications on your Lock screen, they'll be organized by what they are. To see all the notifications from any one category, just tap it.

Not a fan of grouping? No problem. You can turn it off for any app. Head to Settings, then Notifications, then tap the app you want to turn grouping off for. Under Notification Groupings, just turn off automatic.

USING AIRDROP

AirDrop was introduced in iOS 7, though Apple fans have likely used the Mac OS version on MacBooks and iMacs. In Mac OSX Sierra and Yosemite, you'll finally be able to share between iOS and your Mac using AirDrop.

AirDrop is Apple's file sharing service, and it comes standard on iOS 13 devices. You can activate AirDrop from the Share icon anywhere in iOS 13. If other AirDrop users are nearby, you'll see anything they're sharing in AirDrop, and they can see anything you share.

AirDrop. Share instantly with people nearby. If they turn on AirDrop from Control Center on iOS or from Finder on the Mac, you'll see their names here. Just tap to share.

[5]

Now What?

This chapter will cover:
- More about the Phone app
- Sending email
- Surfing the web
- Using iTunes
- Finding apps on the App Store
- Adding calendar items
- Finding the weather
- Using Maps
- Health
- Find My Friends
- Find My Phone
- HomeKit
- ARKit

There are millions of apps you can download, but Apple invests a lot of time making sure some of the best apps are their own. When you get a new iPhone, there are dozens of apps already installed. You're free to delete them (and later download them again), but before you do, make sure you know what they are.

PHONE

In previous chapters, you got a very high-level look at making calls. Now let's go a little deeper.

Open your Phone app. Notice the tabs on the bottom of the screen. Let's go over what each one does.

Favorites: These are the people you call most frequently. They are also in your contacts. It's kind of like your speed dial.

Recent: Any call (outgoing or incoming) will show up here. Incoming calls are in black, and outgoing calls are in red.

Contacts: This is where every contact will be. Do you notice the letters on the side? Tap the letter corresponding to the person you want to call to jump to that letter.

Keypad: This is what you use if you want to call the person using an actual keypad.

Voicemail: all your voicemail is stored here until you erase it.

Personally, I like to add contacts by going to iCloud.com and signing in with my iTunes Account. It automatically syncs with the phone and is web-based which means that it doesn't matter whether you are using a Mac or a PC. I prefer this way because I can type with a real keyboard.

For the sake of this book, however, I am going to use the phone method; which is almost identical to the iCloud.

To add a contact, tap on "Contacts," and then tap the '+' button in the upper right corner. Additionally, you can remove contacts by tapping on the Edit button instead and then tapping on the person you want to delete, then hitting "Delete."

Edit   **Favorites**   +

To insert information, all you need to do is tap in each field. If you tap on "add photo" you will also have the option of taking someone's photo or using one you already have. If you want to assign a ringtone or a vibration, so that it plays a certain song only when this person is calling, then add that under ringtones. When you are finished, tap "Done." It will now give you the option of adding the person to your favorites if this is someone you will call often.

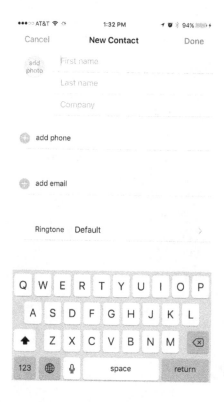

To call any person, simply tap their name. If you want to send them a text message instead, tap the blue arrow to the side of their name. Note that only the blue arrow shows up if in the "Favorites" section. To call someone not in your favorites, tap on their name in contacts and it will ask you if you want to call or text. If you prefer to call the person using Facetime (if they have Facetime) you will also have the option by tapping the blue exclamation button.

One highly advertised feature on the iPhone is Do Not Disturb. When this feature is turned on, no calls get through; you don't even see that your phone is ringing unless it's from someone in your approved list. That way you can have it set to ring only if someone in your family is calling. To use this feature, you need to go to Settings on your Home screen.

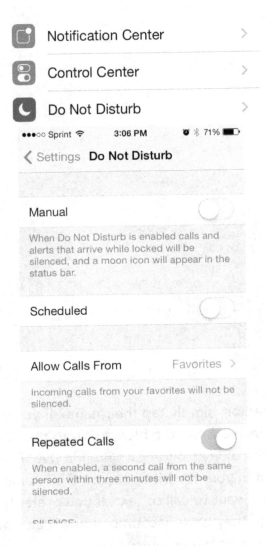

By default, when Do Not Disturb is on, anyone in your favorites can call. Also, notice the Repeated Calls button which is switched on by default. What that means is that if the same person calls twice in three minutes, it will go through.

If you want to set it to let no calls go through, tap on the "Allow Calls From." To get back to the previous menu, just tap the Do Not Disturb button in the upper left corner. Anytime you see a button like that in the upper left corner, it means that it will take you to the previous screen. The information here saves as soon as you tap it, so don't worry about a Save button.

MAIL

The iPhone lets you add multiple email addresses from virtually any email client you can think of. Yahoo, Gmail, AOL, Exchange, Hotmail, and many more can be added to your phone so that you will be able to check your email no matter where you are. To add an email address, click on the Settings app icon, then scroll to the middle where you'll see Mail, Contacts & Calendar. You will then see logos for the biggest email providers, but if you have another type of email just click on "Other" and continue.

If you don't know your email settings, you will need to visit the Mail Settings Lookup page on the Apple website. There you can type in your entire email address, and the website will show you what information to type and where in order to get your email account working on the phone. The settings change with every one, so what works for one provider may not work with another. Once you are finished adding as many email accounts as you may need, you will be able to click on the Mail app icon on your phone's Home screen, and view each inbox separately, or all at once.

SURFING THE INTERNET WITH SAFARI

If you are using the iPhone, you are probably already paying for a data plan, so chances are you want to take full advantage of the Internet.

There's a good chance you are using a carrier that doesn't have unlimited web surfing. This means that if you use the Internet a lot, then you will have to pay extra. What I recommend is using Wi-Fi when you have it (like at home). So, before we go back into Safari, let's look very quickly at how to enable Wi-Fi.

On your Home screen, tap the Settings icon.

The second option in the Settings menu is Wi-Fi; tap anywhere on that line once.

Settings		
✈ Airplane Mode		⬭
📶 Wi-Fi	Off	>
✳ Bluetooth	On	>
📡 Cellular		>

Next, switch the Wi-Fi from off to on by swiping or tapping on the "Off."

Your Wi-Fi network (if you have one) will now appear. Tap it once.

2WIRE103   

If there is a lock next to the signal symbol; that means the Wi-Fi access is locked and you need a password to use it. When prompted, type in the password and then tap "Join."

You will now connect to the network. Remember that many places, like Starbucks, McDonald's, Nordstrom, Lowe's, etc., offer free Wi-Fi as a way to entice you into the store and get you to stay. Take advantage of it and save data usage for the times you need it.

Let's see how Safari works.

Tap the Safari icon once and it will launch. You've already seen how the address bar works. To search for something, you use the same exact box. That's how you can search for anything on the Internet. Think of it like a Google, Bing, or Yahoo! search engine in the corner of your screen. In fact, that's exactly what it is. Because when you search, it will use one of those search engines to find results.

On the bottom of the screen you'll see five buttons; the first two are Back and Forward buttons that make the browser go either backwards or forwards to the website you were previously on.

Next to the forward arrow, right in the middle, is a button that lets you share a website, add it to the Home screen, print it, bookmark it, copy it, or add it to your reading list.

That's great! But what does it all mean? Let's look at each button on the menu:

The first row lets you send the link to your nearby devices or text it to people you often text.

Below that are the apps you can open and send the link to.

Finally, below those are different actions you can take with the link:

Add to Home screen: If you go to a website frequently, this can be very convenient. What this button does is add an icon for that webpage right to your Home screen. That way whenever you want to launch the website, you can do it directly from the Home screen.

Copy: This copies the website address.

Add Bookmark: If you go to a website often but don't want to add it to your Home screen, then you can bookmark it. I will show you this in more detail in just a moment.

Add to Reading List: If you have a bunch of news stories open, you can add them to a reading list to read later (even if you are offline).

The next button over from the share link covered above looks like a book. It is the Bookmark button.

When you add a bookmark (remember you do this from the previous button, the Share one), it will ask you to name it. By default it will put it in the general bookmarks tab, but you can also create new folders by clicking on "Bookmarks."

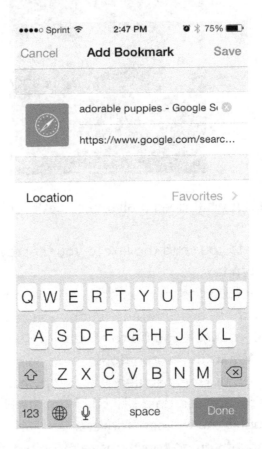

Now you can access the website anytime you want without typing the address by tapping on the Bookmarks button.

> **Bookmarks** Done
>
> | | | |
> |--|--|--|
> | 📖 | ⚬⚬ | @ |
>
> ☆ Favorites   >
>
> 🕐 History   >

Reading List is the middle icon that looks like a pair of glasses where you can view all of the webpages, blog posts, or articles that you've saved for offline reading. To save a piece of internet literature to your reading list, tap on the Share icon and then click on "Add to Reading List." Saved pages can be deleted like a text message by swiping from right to left and tapping on the red Delete button.

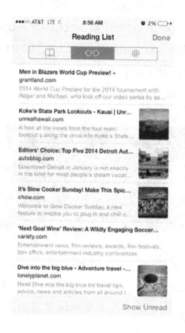

The third tab on the Bookmarks page is where you can view your shared links and subscriptions. Subscriptions can be created from any webpage that provides RSS feeds, and your phone will automatically download the latest articles and posts. To subscribe to a site's RSS, visit the website, tap the Bookmarks icon, and select "Add to Shared Links."

The last button looks like a box on top of a transparent box.

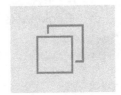

If you use a computer or an iPad; then you probably know all about tabs. Apple decided to not use tabs on Safari. Tabs are there in another way though, that's what this button is; it lets you have several windows open at the same time. When you press it, a new window appears. There's an option to open a new page. Additionally, you can toggle between the pages that you already have opened. Hitting the 'x' will also close a page that you have opened. Hit done to go back to normal browsing.

The iCloud option (the cloud at the bottom) is something you'll want to pay attention to if you use another Apple device (like an iPad, an iPod Touch or a Mac computer). Your Safari browsing is automatically synced; so, if you are browsing a page on your iPad, you can pick up where you left off on your iPhone.

When you put your phone in landscape (i.e. you turn it sideways), the browser also turns, and you will now have the option to use full screen mode. It looks similar, but there's now a '+' button—that lets you open a new Tab.

You can have tabs in both modes, but in full screen you see the tabs on top.

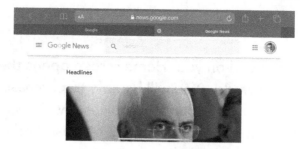

In portrait mode, tabs are seen by tapping the two transparent boxes in the lower right corner.

If you hate closing tabs, your life got easier in iOS 13. You can have all tabs automatically close after a set period of time.

Go to Settings > Safari > Close Tabs and select if you want to do it Manually, After One Day, After One Week, or After One Month.

ITUNES

The iTunes app found on your Home screen opens the biggest digital music store in the world. You will be able to purchase and download not just music, but also countless movies, TV shows, audiobooks, and more. On the iTunes home page, you can also find a What's Hot section, collections of music, and new releases.

At the top, you will see the option to view either featured media or browse through the top charts. On the upper left corner is the Genres button. Clicking "Genres" will bring up many different types of music to help refine your search.

BUYING APPS

So how do you buy, download and finally remove apps? I'll look at that in this section.

To purchase apps (and I don't actually mean paying for them because you can purchase a free app without paying for it):

The first thing you see when you open the App Store is the Today screen.

This is a little different than the App Store you may be familiar with from older OS's. Apple gave it a more magazine look where you discover apps based on editor-curated lists.

The bottom has tabs to discover games, apps, arcade (a new Apple service), and search for apps. If you want to see app categories, then go to Apps and scroll a little. See All will show you all.

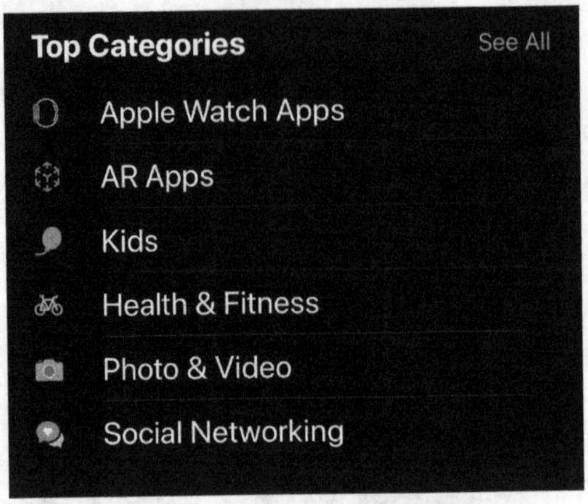

Top Categories   See All

◯   Apple Watch Apps

⬡   AR Apps

🌰   Kids

🚲   Health & Fitness

📷   Photo & Video

💬   Social Networking

To update apps, you used to tap on the last tab, which would say update. That option is gone. The easiest way to update apps is to have the auto update option turned on at setup. To manually update an app, or see if it was recently updated, tap your avatar photo in the upper right corner. This brings up your account information and updates available (if it says "open" that means it was recently updated; if it says "update" that means there's an update available).

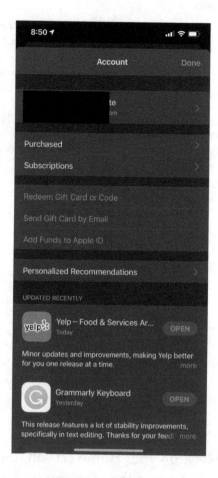

If you bought an app, but accidentally deleted it, or changed your mind about deleting it, don't worry! You can download the app again in the same place that you see the updates. Just tap on "Purchased."

When you tap the Purchased button, you will see two options: one is to see all the apps you have purchased, and one to see just the apps that you have purchased but are not on your phone. Tap the one that says "Not on This iPhone" to re-download anything, at no cost. Just tap the Cloud button to the right of the screen. You can even download it again if you bought it on another iPhone as long as it's under the same account.

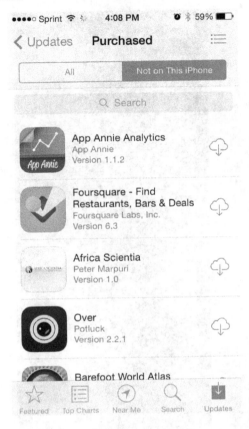

Deleting apps is easy; on your Home screen, tap and hold the icon of the app you want to remove, then tap the 'x' on top of the app.

CALENDAR

Among the other pre-installed apps that came with your new iPhone, perhaps one of the most used apps you'll encounter is the Calendar. You can switch between viewing appointments, tasks, or everything laid out in a one-day, one-week, or one-month view. Turn your phone on its side and you will notice everything switch to landscape mode. A first for the iPhone, many new apps now take advantage of the larger iPhone's 1080p resolution by displaying more information at once, similar to the iPad and iPad mini display. Combine your calendar with email accounts or iCloud to keep your appointments and tasks synced across all of your devices, and never miss another appointment.

Creating an Appointment

To create an appointment, click on the Calendar icon on your Home screen. Click on whichever day you would like to set the appointment for, and then tap the '+' button in the corner. Here you will be able to name and edit your event, as well as connect it to an email or iCloud account in order to allow for syncing.

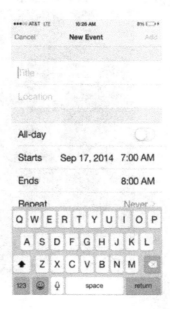

When editing your event, pay special attention to the duration of your event. Select the start and end times, or choose "All Day" if it's an all-day event. You will also have a chance to set it as a recurring event by clicking on "Repeat" and selecting how often you want it to repeat. In the case of a bill or car payment, for example, you could either select Monthly (on this day) or every 30 days, which are two different things. After you select your repetition, you can also choose how long you'd like that event to repeat itself: for just one month, a year, forever, and everything in between.

A recent update to Calendar now let's you include attachments to your appointments; you can add an attachment by selecting "Add Attachment" at the bottom of the New Event screen.

WEATHER

You can use your iPhone's location services and GPS to help you navigate to your destinations, but other apps can also use them to display localized information. The Weather app is one such example of this. Opening it up will immediately show you basic weather information based on your current location. To get more detailed information, you can swipe left and right on the middle section to scroll through the hourly forecast, and swipe up and down on the bottom section to scroll through the 10 day forecast.

You can add more cities by clicking on the list icon towards the bottom right and searching for the city name. Once you've added cities, you can scroll between cities to see real-time weather information for each location by swiping left or right, and the number of cities you have added are shown at the bottom in the form of small dots.

MAPS

The Maps app is back and better than ever. After Apple parted ways with Google Maps several years ago, Apple decided to develop its own, made-for-iPhone map and navigation system. The result is a beautiful travel guide that takes full advantage of the newest iPhone resolutions. Full screen mode allows every corner of the phone to be filled with the app, and there's an automatic night mode. You'll be able to search for places, restaurants, gas stations, concert halls, and other venues near you at any time, and turn-by-turn navigation is available for walking, biking, driving, or commuting. Traffic is updated in real time, so if an accident occurs ahead of you or there is construction going on, Maps will offer a faster alternative and warn you of the potential traffic jam.

The turn-by-turn navigation is easy to understand without being distracting, and the 3D view makes potentially difficult scenarios (like highway exits that come up abruptly) much more pleasant. Another convenient feature is the ability to avoid highways and toll roads entirely.

To set up navigation, tap on the Maps icon. On the bottom of the screen is a search for place or address; for homes you need an address, but businesses just need a name. Click on it and enter your destination once prompted.

When you find your destination's address, click on "Route," and choose between walking or driving directions. For businesses, you also have the option of reading reviews and calling the company directly.

For hands-free navigation, press and hold the Side button to enable Siri (which will be discussed in the next section) and say, "Navigate to..." or "Take me to..." followed by the address or name of the location that you'd like to go to.

If you'd like to avoid highways or tolls, simply tap the More Options button and select the option that you want.

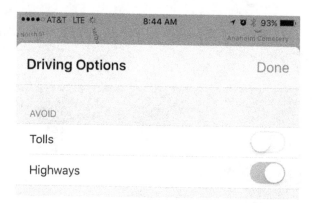

Apple Maps also lets you see a 3D view of thousands of locations. To enable this option, tap the 'i' in the upper right corner. After this, select satellite view.

If 3D view is available you'll notice a change immediately. You can use two fingers to make your map more or less flat. You can also select 2D to remove 3D altogether.

Switch back to the normal map and you will see a little magnifying glass in the upper right corner.

Google has Street View, Apple Map now has a competitor called Look Around (hint, you have to zoom in a little to see it). You won't see this option in every city yet, but you probably will soon. With Look Around on, you can drag the magnifying glass anywhere you want to see a ground view.

When you tap inside the search bar, you'll also notice two newer areas:

- Favorites—which are just places you frequently go.
- Collections—this is where you can create several locations and group them together. So, for example, you might be planning a trip to Europe; you could create a list of all the places you want to see in a collection and jump to them when you are in the city.

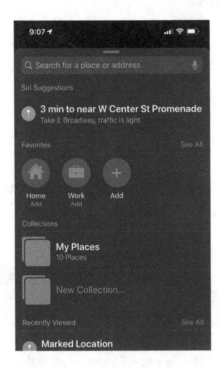

HEALTH

The release of the latest iPhone models brought with it a much greater focus on one's health, and as such, the new iPhones come with the Health app. The Health app keeps track of many different things pertaining to your health, including calories burned, your weight, heart rate, body measurements, and even an emergency card that lets you store important health information such as your blood type and allergies in the event of an emergency. iOS 13 also added a cycle tracker.

FIND MY

If you used Find My Phone or Find My Friend on previous OS's, then shocker: they're gone! These two powerful apps let you see where your friends were on a map or where your devices were on a map.

They're essentially the same app with a different purpose; so instead of keeping both, Apple decided to delete them and combine them into one app called Find My.

The app is pretty simple. Three tabs on the bottom. One to find your friends (i.e. People), one to find your devices, and one to change settings (i.e. Me).

If you want to see where your friend is at, ask them to share their location with you in the People section.

It's not very helpful using an app to find your iPhone if you don't have your iPhone. If that's the case, you can also use your computer browser to see it at iCloud.com.

REMINDERS

The Reminders App has been on iOS for a long time; in iOS 13, however, the app got a facelift. Creating lists is now more visual, intuitive, and it's now easier to share and collaborate.

To get started, tap the Reminders icon.

Creating a list is still very simple. Tap Add List from the lower right corner of your screen.

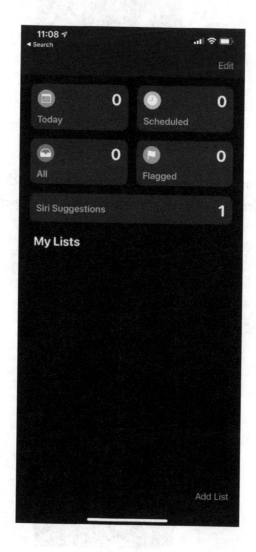

Once you create a list, you can change the color of the icon that represents the list, and rename the list; tap Done to save it.

Once you create your first list, you can start adding to it by tapping Add Reminders from the bottom left corner of the screen.

Tap Return on your keyboard to add another item, or Done when you have added everything (you can add more later).

If you tap the ⓘ at any point, you'll be able to add more details (such as a due date or even what location to remind you at—you could, for example, have it remind you when you get to the grocery store).

Tapping on the three dots in the upper right corner brings up additional list options. In addition to changing things like the name, you can add people to the list so they can collaborate and add things of their own.

To remove or flag a list item, just swipe over it to the left.

Swiping to the list on the previous screen will also let you delete an entire list.

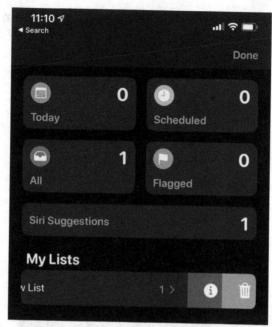

From the main list menu, you can select Edit in the upper right corner and organize the order of your lists.

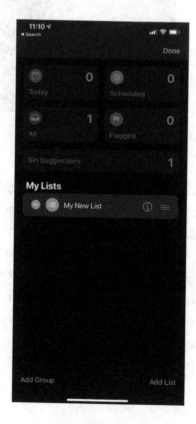

In this edit mode, you can also select Add Group and group different lists together.

HOME

The Home app integrates HomeKit with iOS to help you better integrate all your home appliances and utilities, like lights, thermostats, refrigerators, and more. HomeKit uses Siri to control all of your smart home devices, which is a pretty handy tool, and the Home interface allows for a much cleaner and straightforward experience. To add your smart home device to Home, simply stand next to it with its power on and your Home app enabled. You can also use your 4th generation Apple TV to control HomeKit-enabled smart home devices. HomePod is something else that is housed here.

ARKIT

iPhone is all about augmented reality; they see this as the future. Many new apps have AR support.

New Feature Alert: ARKit for iOS 12 introduced a new measurements tool. That's still there in iOS 13.

To use the new measurements tool, open the Measure app. Point your camera at a rectangle option, and watch a box automatically form over it.

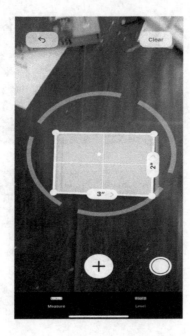

The app will tell you how long something is, and also allow you to add points, so you can measure it as well.

[6]

CUSTOMIZE

This chapter will cover:
- Screen Time
- Do Not Disturb Mode
- Notifications and Widgets
- General Settings
- Sounds
- Customizing Brightness and Wallpaper
- Adding Facebook, Twitter and Flickr Accounts
- Family Sharing
- Continuity and Handoff

Now that you know your way around, it's time to dig into the settings and make this phone completely custom to you!

For most of this chapter, I'll be hanging out in the Settings area, so if you aren't already there, tap Settings from your Home screen.

To use Screen Time, head on into Settings > Screen Time

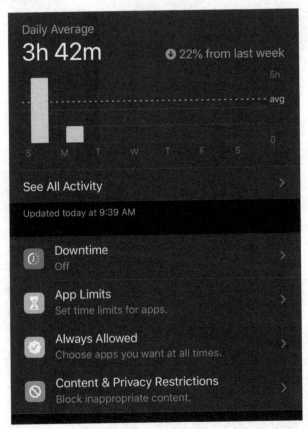

You can click on any app to see how much time you've spent in it, and even what your average is. From here you can also add limits.

DO NOT DISTURB MODE

Do Not Disturb mode is a handy feature located near the top of your Settings app. When this operational mode is enabled, you won't receive any notifications and all of your calls will be silenced. This is a useful trick for those times when you can't afford to be distracted (and let's face it, your iPhone is as communicative as they come, and sometimes you'll need to have some peace and quiet!). Clock alarms will still sound.

To turn on, schedule and customize Do Not Disturb, just tap on "Do Not Disturb" in Settings. You can schedule automatic times to activate this feature, like your work hours, for example. You can also specify certain callers who should be allowed when your phone is set to Do Not Disturb. This way your mother can still get through, but you won't have to hear every incoming email. To do this, use the Allow Call From command in Do Not Disturb settings.

Do Not Disturb is also accessible through the Control Center (swipe down from the upper right corner of the screen to access it at any time).

NOTIFICATIONS AND WIDGETS

Notifications are one of the most useful features on the iPhone, but chances are you won't need to be informed of every single event that's set as a default in your Notifications Center. To adjust Notifications preferences, go to Settings > Notifications.

By tapping the app, you can turn notifications off or on and finesse the type of notification from each app. It's a good idea to whittle this list down to the apps that you truly want to be notified from—for example, if you're not an investor, turn off Stocks! Reducing the number of sounds your iPhone makes can also reduce phone-related frazzledness. For example, in Mail, you may want your phone to make a sound when you receive email from someone on your VIP list, but to only display badges for other, less important email.

GENERAL SETTINGS

The General menu item is a little bit of a catchall. This is where you'll find information about your iPhone, including its current version of iOS and any available software updates. Fortunately, iOS 13 ushers in an era of smaller, more efficient updates, so you won't find yourself scrambling to delete apps in order to make space for the latest improvements.

The Accessibility options are located here as well. You can set your iPhone according to your needs with Zoom, VoiceOver, large text, color adjustment, and more. There are quite a few Accessibility options that can make iOS 13 easy for everyone to use, including Grayscale View and improved Zoom options.

A handy Accessibility option that's a little disguised is the Assistive Touch setting. This gives you a menu that helps you access device-level functions. Enabling it brings up a floating menu designed to help users who have difficulty with screen gestures like swiping, or with manipulating the iPhone's physical buttons. Another feature for those with visual needs is Magnifier. Turning this on allows your camera to magnify things.

I recommend taking some time and tapping through the General area, just so you know where everything is!

CELLULAR

If you are worried about Data caps, you can change the data settings to reduce the data used. Go to Settings > Cellular > Cellular Data Options and then check off Low Data Mode.

SOUNDS

Hate that vibration when your phone rings? Want to change your ring tone? Head to the Sounds Settings menu! Here you can turn vibration on or off and assign ring tones to a number of iPhone functions. I do suggest finding an isolated space before you start trying out all the different sound settings—it's fun, but possibly a major annoyance to those unlucky enough not to be playing with their own new iPhone!

Tip: You can apply individual ringtones and message alerts to your contacts. Just go to the person's contact screen in Contacts, tap "Edit," and tap "Assign Ringtone."

Swipe Keyboard

A Swipe Keyboard was added in iOS 13. What's that? Instead of lifting your finger as you tap, you swipe across the keyboard. Some people prefer it and feel like they can type faster using it. Others can't stand it. If you want to try it out, go to Settings > General > Keyboard.

Customizing Brightness and Wallpaper

On the iPhone, wallpaper refers to the background image on your Home screen and to the image displayed when your iPhone is locked (Lock screen). You can change either image using two methods.

For the first method, visit Settings > Wallpapers. You'll see a preview of your current wallpaper and Lock screen here. Tap "Choose a New Wallpaper." From there, you can choose a pre-loaded dynamic (moving) or still image, or choose one of your own photos. Once you've chosen an image, you'll see a preview of the image as a Lock screen. Here, you can turn off Perspective Zoom (which makes the image appear to shift as you tilt your phone) if you like. Tap "Set" to continue. Then choose whether to set the image as the Lock screen, Home screen, or both.

The other way to make the change is through your Photos app. Find the photo you'd like to set as a wallpaper image and tap the Share button. You'll be given a choice to set an image as a background, a Lock screen, or both.

If you want to use images from the web, it's fairly easy. Just press and hold the image until the Save Image / Copy / Cancel message comes up. Saving the image will save it to your Recently Added photos in the Photos app.

PRIVACY

The Privacy heading in Settings lets you know what apps are doing with your data. Every app you've allowed to use Location Services will show up under Location Services (and you can toggle Location Services off and on for individual apps or for your whole device here as well). You can also go through your apps to check what information each one is receiving and transmitting.

MAIL, CONTACTS, CALENDARS SETTINGS

If you need to add additional mail, contacts or calendar accounts, tap Settings > Mail, Contacts and Calendars to do so. It's more or less the same process as adding a new account in-app. You can also adjust other settings here, including your email signature for each linked account. This is also a good place to check which aspects of each account are linked—for example, you may want to link your Tasks, Calendars and Mail from Exchange, but not your Contacts. You can manage all of this here.

There are a number of other useful settings here, including the frequency you want your accounts to check for mail (Push, the default, being the hardest on your battery life). You can also turn on features like Ask Before Deleting and adjust the day of the week you'd like your calendar to start on.

ADDING FACEBOOK AND TWITTER

If you use Twitter, Facebook or Flickr, you'll probably want to integrate them with your iPhone. This is a snap to do. Just tap on Settings and look for Twitter, Facebook and Flickr in the main menu (you can also integrate Vimeo and Weibo accounts if you have them). Tap on the platform you want to integrate. From there, you'll enter your user name and password. Doing this will allow you to share webpages, photos, notes, App Store pages, music and more, straight from your iPhone's native apps.

iPhone will ask you if you'd like to download the free Facebook, Twitter and Flickr apps when you configure your accounts if you haven't already done so. I recommend doing this—the apps are easy to use, free, and look great.

I found that when I associated my Facebook account, my contact list got extremely bloated. If you don't want to include your Facebook friends in your contacts list, adjust the list of applications that can access your Contacts in Settings > Facebook.

FAMILY SHARING

Family Sharing is one of my favorite iOS 13 features. Family Sharing allows you to share App Store and iTunes purchases with family members (previously, accomplishing this required a tricky and not-entirely-in-compliance-with-terms-of-service dance). Turning on Family Sharing also creates a shared family calendar, photo album, and reminder list. Family members can also see each other's location in Apple's free Find My ap. Overall, Family Sharing is a great way to keep everyone entertained and in sync! You can include up to six people in Family Sharing.

To enable Family Sharing, go to Settings > iCloud. Here, tap "Set Up Family Sharing" to get started. The person who initiates Family Sharing for a family is known as the family organizer. It's an important role, since every purchase made by family members will be made using the family organizer's credit card! Once you set up your family, they'll also be able to download your past purchases, including music, movies, books, and apps.

Invite your family members to join Family Sharing by entering their Apple IDs. As a parent, you can create Apple IDs for your children with parental consent. When you create a new child Apple ID, it is automatically added to Family Sharing.

There are two types of accounts in Family Sharing—adult and child. As you'd expect, child accounts have more potential restrictions than adult accounts do. Of special interest is the Ask to Buy option. This prevents younger family members from running up the family organizer's credit card bill by requiring parental authorization for purchases. The family organizer can also designate other adults in the family as capable of authorizing purchases on children's devices.

CONTINUITY AND HANDOFF

iOS 13 includes some incredible features for those of us who work on multiple iOS 13 and OSX devices. Now, when your computer is running Yosemite or higher, or your iOS 13 iPad is connected to the same Wi-Fi network as your iOS 13 iPhone, you can answer calls or send text messages (both iMessages and regular SMS messages) from your iPad or computer.

The Handoff feature is present in apps like Numbers, Safari, Mail and many more. Handoff allows you to leave an app in one device mid-action and pick up right where you left off on a different device. It makes life much easier for those of us living a multi-gadget lifestyle.

[7]

TAKING PICTURES

This chapter will cover:
- Taking photos and videos
- Editing photos
- Sharing and organizing photos / videos

TAKING PHOTOS

Now that you know your way around some of the settings, let's get back to the fun stuff! I'll look at using the Camera app next.

The Camera app is on your Home screen, but you can also access it from your Lock screen for quick, easy access.

The Camera app is pretty simple to use. First, you should know that the Camera app has two cameras: one on the front and one on the back.

The front camera has typically had a lower resolution and was mostly used for self-portraits; with the iPhone 11 and iPhone Pro, the front camera was upgraded to 12 MP and takes the same pro photos as the back. All the features covered in this section are on both the front- and back-facing cameras with the exception of Time-Lapse and Pano modes.

There are six modes on the camera. When you launch the app, you'll see the different modes at the bottom just above the shutter. Use your finger to slide to the mode you want; the mode in yellow is the mode that is active.

SE   SLO-MO   VIDEO   **PHOTO**   PORTRAIT   PANO

The six modes are as follows:
- Time-Lapse – Time-lapsed videos
- Slow-Mo – Slow-motion videos
- Video
- Photo (the default mode)
- Portrait – For studio-like photos that give a blurred background effect
- Pano – For panoramic photos

USING THE LENES

The iPhone Pro comes with three lenses:
- Ultra-wide
- Wide
- Telephoto

When you take a normal photo or video (not portrait or slo-mo video) you will see three numbers: .5, 1x, and 2. These represent the lens. Tapping them will make the preview either zoom in or out.

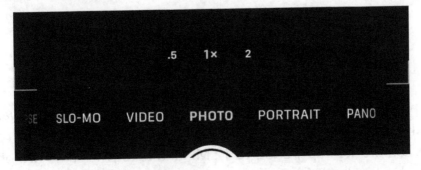

If you tap and hold one of the numbers, you'll get more precise numbers—so if you don't want to zoom all the way in or out, you don't have to. You can also pinch in and out on your screen to zoom in and out.

What does all this mean in practice? To give you an example, below are three photos taken at the same spot with each lens.

Ultra-Wide (0.5)

Wide (1x)

Telephoto (2)

DIFFERENT CAMERA MODES

At the top of the app are three buttons: flash, night mode, and live mode. Night mode comes on automatically in low-light settings.

Tapping on the arrow in the middle of this will give you an expanded list of options.

The options appear at the bottom after you expand it. The options are as follows: flash, night mode, live mode, frame, timer, and color.

If you tap on any of these options you get more options to either toggle them on and off or, when applicable, make adjustments to them.

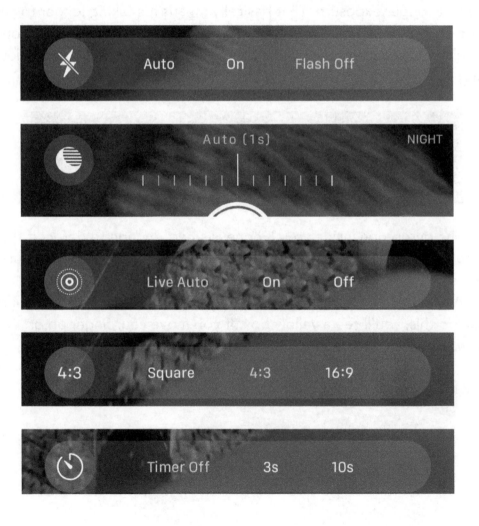

Night Mode is a new feature on the iPhone 11 and Pro, and the manual controls here might seem a little unfamiliar; Night Mode will come on automatically (if activated, the icon will be yellow and indicate the number of seconds it will shoot for), but when you press the Night Mode icon, you can manually adjust the settings it would automatically capture.

What Night Mode is doing automatically behind the scenes is simulating a longer exposure. That basically means it's taking longer to capture the image. The slider in Night Mode adjust the number of seconds it will be exposed—the longer it's exposed the more light you are letting in.

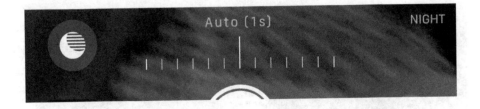

The gyroscope inside your iPhone is smart enough to detect if the iPhone is resting on a tripod. If it is, it will allow for even longer exposures.

As you take a photo, you can tap a person or object to focus on. As you do this, you'll see a yellow box. If you move your finger up or down, it will adjust the brightness of the photo.

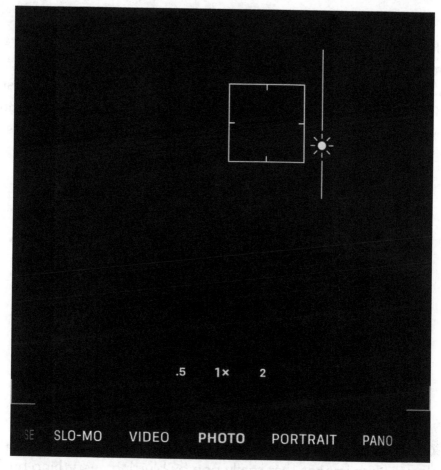

As you take photos, you can capture quick videos without leaving the photo. Tap and hold the shutter and drag it to the right, then release it when you are done recording the quick video. This effect can also be performed when you are shooting a video and want a quick photo.

BURST MODE

Previous iPhones let you take a "Burst" of photos by holding the shutter; this was ideal for things like action shots—you could take dozens of photos in seconds and then later pick the one you like best.

Holding the shutter not lets you slide to take a quick video. Burst, however, can still be accomplished. The new method is tapping shutter and sliding your finger to the left.

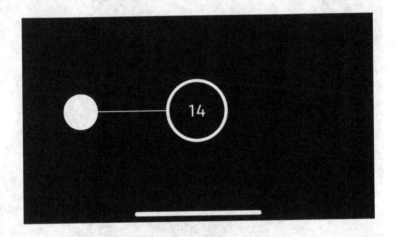

Portrait Mode

One of the most popular camera modes is portrait mode. Portrait mode captures images that really pop by blurring everything but the subject.

When you drag your finger over the boxes just above Portrait, you can see all the different modes within Portrait mode. They are: Natural Light, Studio Light, Contour Light, Stage Light, Stage Light Mono, and High-Key Light Mono.

When you take a Portrait photo, you can change the mode when you edit the photo. So, for example, if you take it with Studio Light, but decide later that you want Natural Light, it won't be too late to change it. I'll cover this in the next section.

Pano Mode

Pano mode lets you patch several photos together to create one giant landscape photo. You can switch lenses before taking the photo.

QR CODES

Have you ever seen one of those boxes on a business telling you to scan it for more information? That's a QR Code.

In the past, you would need an app to open that. iPhone's native camera now has that function built in. Hold up your phone to a QR Code and act like you are going to take a picture. As soon as it focuses on it, a drop-down notification will appear asking you if you'd like to open the link Safari.

EDITING PHOTOS

Now that you've captured your masterpiece, you'll want to edit it to really make it shine. There are thousands of photo editor apps on the App Store. Some, like Adobe Lightroom, will let you make professional changes to the photos, while others are just for fun.

For this chapter, I'm going to stick to making basic edits with Apple's built-in editor. This isn't to say the edits won't be professional—or even fun; there's a lot you can do with the editor.

Regular and Live Photos

The options in editor change based on the kind of photo you took. If you took a Live photo, then there will be a few extra edits you can do; the same is true if you captured in Portrait mode. This first section is going to cover the most common photos: regular (non-Live) and Live.

How do you know what kind of photo it is? When you go into the photos app and view the photo, it will tell you right below the back arrow in the upper left corner. The below example is a Live photo.

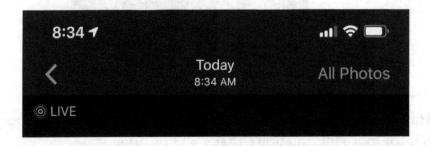

At the bottom of the photo is a list of all options available for editing the photo. The first is the Export button. This option lets you alter the photo outside of the photo app. What does that mean? For starters, you can share via text, email, AirDrop, or upload it to another app, but there's a lot more you can do here: print, add to Wallpaper, add to an album, assign to a contact, and more. The next option is the favorite button (I'll cover where these photos go in the next section); the last options are to Edit and Delete the photo.

When you select Edit, you'll see several new options on the bottom in the Now Open photo editor. The first option is the Live button (if it's a Live photo). When you take a Live photo, you'll have several photos within that photo; by tapping on the Live button, you can select the photo you want to use. The phone automatically picks what it believes is the best photo, but this isn't always the case.

Next to the Live button is the option to make corrections to the photo's overall look. The first option is to Autocorrect (this adjusts the lighting and color levels to what the phone believes is best). Next to that are all the manual corrections: Exposure, Brilliance, Highlights, Shadows, Contrast, Brightness, Black Point, Saturation, Vibrance, Warmth, Tint, Sharpness, Definition, Noise Reduction, and Vignette.

As you slide your finger to the correction you want to perform, you'll notice a slider bar beneath it; you use your finger to move left and right to define the intensity of the correction.

Next is the option to apply Filters to the photos. This works in a similar way: select the filter you want to apply, and then use the slider below to increase or decrease the intensity of the filter. The available filters are Vivid, Vivid Warm, Vivid Cool, Dramatic, Dramatic Warm, Dramatic Cool, Mono, Silvertone, and Noir.

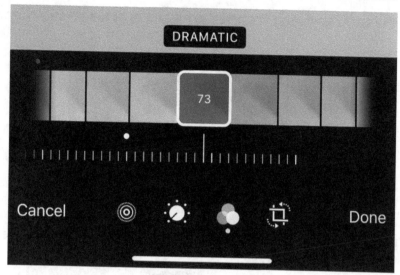

The last option is to Crop. Notice, when you select this option, there are small, white, corner lines around the photo? You can use these to drag to the areas you want to crop—slide in and out, up and down, or left and right.

At the bottom of the cropped area are options to straighten the photo.

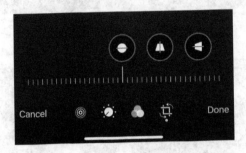

In the top left corner are options to rotate or flip the photo.

The top right has options to crop to a pre-defined size.

When you select the pre-defined size button, you'll see several new options; these are helpful if you are creating for something in particular—like a frame.

When you finish all your edits, tap the Done button; additionally, you can undo everything and keep the original photo by selecting Cancel.

At any point, you can also tap the three dots in the upper right corner of the screen. This brings up the options menu.

If you have other photo apps, you might see them here; the option most people will likely use, however, is the Markup option.

Markup lets you draw and add shapes to the photo—think of it like note taking on a photo.

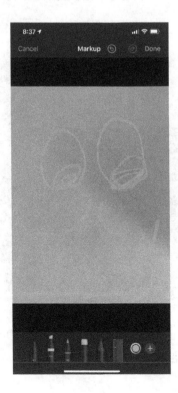

The bottom has all your choices for color and writing instrument. You can also use the ruler to help you draw a straight line with any of those choices.

You can additionally tap the plus button to add shapes, text, a signature, and more.

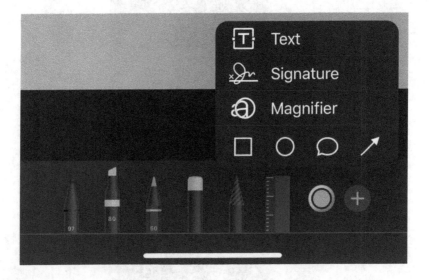

Once you're done with the Markups, tap Done to save your creation or Cancel to erase everything.

Portrait Photos

Editing a portrait photo is exactly the same—with a few exceptions covered in this section.

You know it's a Portrait photo by the indication at the top of the photo.

Once you tap that you want to edit the photo, select the first button, which brings up the Portrait edits available. Use your finger to slide to the Portrait edit you want to make to the photo. Available filters are Natural Light, Studio Light, Contour Light, Stage Light, Stage Light Mono, and High-Key Light Mono. Once you make the filter selection, a slider appears below it to adjust the intensity of it.

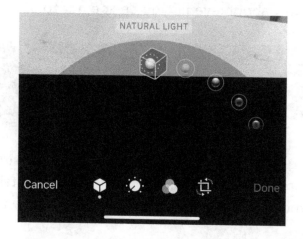

In the upper left corner of the screen, you'll see a button that says f 4.5; this option adjusts the depth of the photo (or the background blur).

When you tap this option, you'll see a slider appear at the bottom of your screen where you can adjust the depth of the photo.

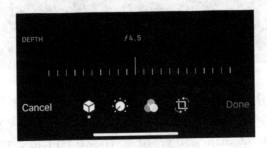

CAMERA SETTINGS YOU SHOULD KNOW

If you go into you Settings, then Camera, there are several settings you should know about (even if you decide not to use them right now).

The setting that I believe is most useful is Composition. Toggling on Photos Capture Outside the Frame means when you take a photo, you can capture more than what you see when you thumb through all of your photos.

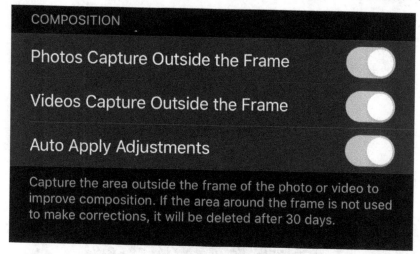

What does that mean? Look at the image below. The image in the center is what I see in my library, but when I go to Edit and Crop, notice how the area is larger? I can drag over to show even more of the photo.

If you don't like that the camera goes back to the default settings whenever you open it, then you can toggle on the Preserve settings.

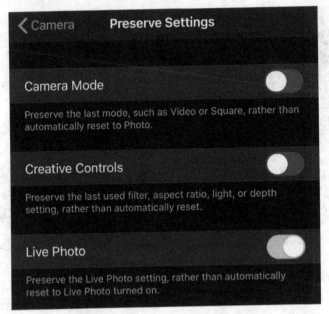

When you record a video, you can shoot as high as 4K. However, doing so creates very large videos. You can record in a lower setting. Tap on Record Video to update your preferences.

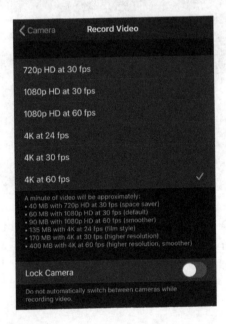

You can also change the Slow-mo camera settings.

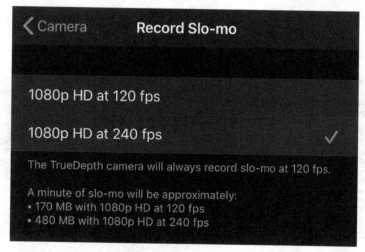

Finally, toggling on Grid will put a grid over your photo app to help you take straight photos and videos.

Viewing, Organizing, Searching and Sharing Photos

Now that you have made changes to your photos, how do you find and organize them? This section will cover that.

When you open the Photos app, there are four tabs available: Photos (where you see all photos), For You (curated collections of photos—like On This Day memories), Albums (where private shared albums live), Search (where you search for your photos).

Viewing Photos
When you select the first tab (Photos) you'll notice a new option appears at the bottom: Years, Months, Days, All Photos. If you are like most people, you probably have thousands and thousands of photos

on your phone. This just makes it easier to find what you are looking for.

It also makes it easier to share memories. For example, if I want to share all the photos I took on New Year's Day with my wife. I just go to Years, and go to the year I want, then slide to Months, and find January. Slide again to Days and find January First, and finally in the top right corner tap the tree dots to bring up the options for the photos. This collects all the photos together and gives me a few options: Share them, put them in a movie, or show them on a map.

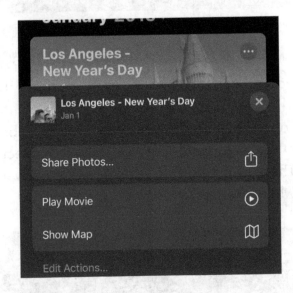

When I select share, it asks me how I want to share them, and I just pick Messages to text my wife the pictures.

From here, they are all assigned an iCloud link, and that link is inserted into a text message. When my wife gets it, she won't see fifty-one photos appear; she'll see a photo with a link to the location for all. That way she can either view them, download them, or select only a few photos to download.

For You

You probably noticed by now that your phone is pretty smart. It has all sorts of things running in the background to figure out who you are and what you like; For You is one area that shows this off. It recognizes when you take a lot of photos in a particular area and marks them as memories, then starts assigning them to this section. You can do all the things you did in Photos, such as share them and turn them into movies.

Not all memories are happy ones; when you open up memories, you can tap the options in the upper right corner to either block or delete a memory.

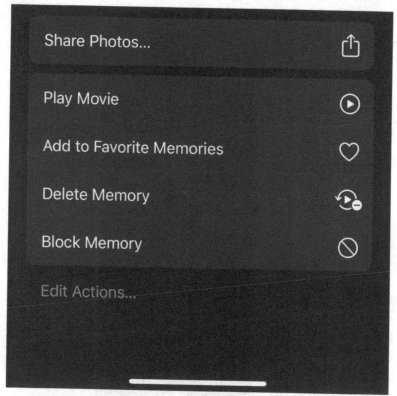

If you decide to play a movie with the memory (and this also applies to any album you turn into a movie), you can edit how it will show—a short or medium clip, and what kind of effects (like music) it has.

Albums

Albums is where you can really start to organize things. Remember when I said above that when you press the like button on a photo it goes to the Favorites folder. This is where you'll find that folder. To add an album, tap the **+** button.

This will ask if you want to create a New Album or New Shared Album; the first option is something you see and the second is something you make available to others.

When you create a Shared Album, it will first ask you to give it a name.

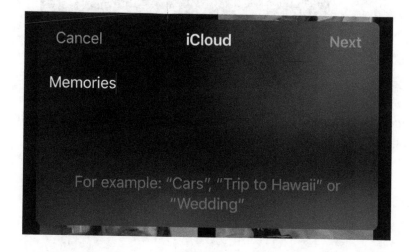

Next, you select who you want to share it with (you can also leave it blank for now).

After this you'll see a blank shared album.

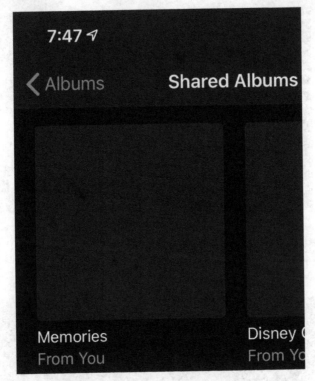

Once you tap on the album, you can start adding your photos.

Selecting People on the bottom allows you to invite people to view it. Under People, you'll also see settings to let people share photos to the album—so, for example, if you just had a wedding, you can share an album with everyone that was there and ask them to add in all of the photos they took. You also go to People to delete an album.

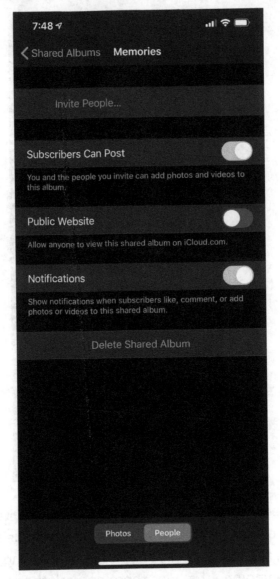

At any time, you can also go into People and tap a person's name who is a member of the album and remove them.

Search

Search is pretty smart. You may wonder how you can search for photos when there is no text. There are a number of ways.

When you take a photo, it geotags the location (in other words, it labels where it was taken—either the city or in some cases the actual name of a place; for example, if you were at a museum, then it would know the name of the museum based on the geotag).

Another way is through facial recognition. When you take a photo, the AI inside your phone scans it to see if it notices a person or even an animal.

One of the first things you see when you tap the search option is People; in the example below, I can tap on Dad and see all the photos I've taken that have my dad in them; I can also search in the box above for a location and Dad, which would find any photo of my dad at that location.

To give you an example, I go to Disneyland a lot because I live in Southern California and have a kid. When I search Disneyland, it will show me every photo I've taken there—over 6,000! Like I said, I go there a lot.

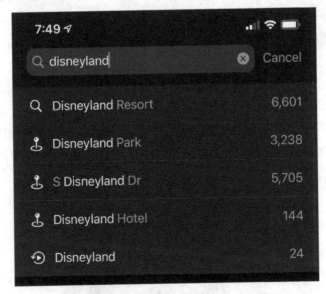

Because there are so many results, I can start adding other things to the search. For example, I can search for Nashville, and then I can also search for just photos with food in them, or just photos taken in the Winter.

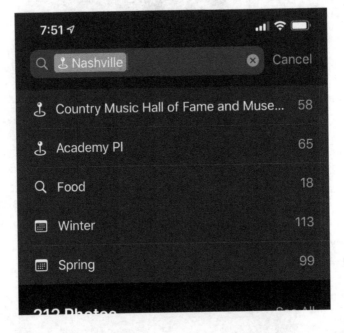

The search isn't quite as smart when it comes to other things, but it's evolving. It can detect objects, for example, but not quite as accurately as people. It does do a pretty good job with animals, however.

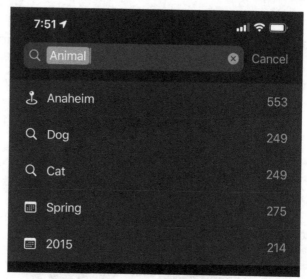

When there is a person it notices in a lot of your photos, it will come up as Unnamed Person; once you give the person a name, it will start showing all photos with that person with that name.

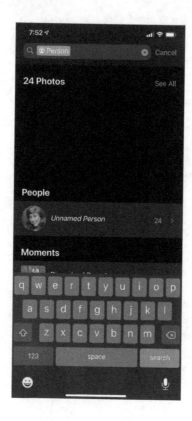

When you tap on a person, you can select the options in the upper right corner to see further options; you can share the photos, turn them into a movie, and more. There's also an option to confirm additional photos, which lets you see photos the AI might not be too sure about.

[8]

ANIMOJI

This chapter will cover:
- What is Animoji?
- How to use Animoji

HOW TO ADD YOUR OWN ANIMOJI

I'm going to be honest, I think Animoji is a little creepy—but also fun! What is it? You almost have to try it to understand it. In a nutshell, Animoji turns you into an emoji. Want to send someone an emoji of a monkey? That's fun. But you know else is fun? Making that monkey have the same expression as you!

When you use Animoji, you put the camera in front of you. If you put out your tongue, the emoji sticks out it's tongue. If you wink, the emoji winks. So, it's a way to send a person an emoji with exactly how you are feeling.

To use it, open your iMessage app. Start a text the way you normally would. Tap the App button followed by the Animoji button. Choose an Animoji and tap to see full screen. Look directly into the camera and place your face into the fame. Tap the Record button and speak for up to 10 seconds. Tap the Preview button to look at the Animoji. Tap the Upward Arrow button to send or the Trashcan to delete.

You can also create an emoji that looks like you. Click that big '+' button next to the other Animojis.

This will walk you through all the steps to send your very own custom Animoji—from hair color to type of nose.

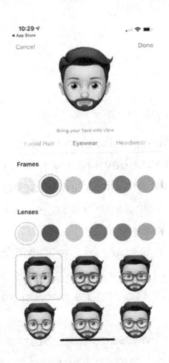

When you're done, you are ready to send.

You can now use Animojis as your profile photo in Messages. Go to Settings > Messages, then select Share Name and Photo.

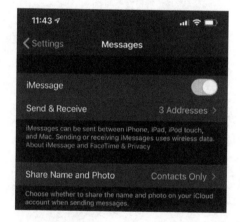

From here, select Edit under your avatar, select your photo, and then allow it to be used.

[9]

HEY, SIRI

This chapter will cover:
- Siri

By now, you probably know all about Siri and how she can remind you of things. If not, press and hold the Side button.

So, what exactly do you do with it? The first thing you should do is introduce Siri to your family. Siri is pretty smart, and she wants to meet your family. To introduce her to your family, activate Siri by pressing and holding the Home button and say: "Brian is my brother" or "Susan is my boss." Once you confirm the relationship you can now say things like: "Call my brother" or "Email my boss."

Siri is also location-based. What does that mean? It means that instead of saying, "Remind me to call wife at 8 AM" you can say, "Remind me when I leave work to call wife," and as soon as you step out of the office you will receive a reminder. Siri can be a bit frustrating at first, but it's one of the phone's most powerful apps, so give it a chance!

Everyone hates to deal with waiting. There's nothing worse than being hungry and having to wait an hour for a table. Siri does her best to make your life easier by making reservations for you. For this to work, you'll need a free app called "OpenTable" (you'll also need a free account), which is in the Apple App store. This app makes its money from restaurants paying it, so don't worry about having to pay to use it. Once it's installed, you will simply activate Siri (press the Home button until it turns on) and say, "Siri, make me a reservation at the Olive Garden," (or wherever you want to eat). Note that not all restaurants participate in OpenTable, but hundreds (if not thousands) do, and it's growing monthly, so if it's not there, it probably will be soon.

Siri is ever evolving. And with the latest update, Apple has taught her everything she needs to know about sports. Go ahead, try it! Press and hold the 'Home' button to activate Siri, and then say something like: "What's the score in the Kings game" or: "Who leads the league in homeruns?"

Siri has also gotten a little wiser in movies. You can say, "Movies directed by Peter Jackson" and it will give you a list and let you see a synopsis, the review rating from Rotten Tomatoes, and in some cases even a trailer or an option to buy the movie. You can also say, "Movie show times" and nearby movies that are playing will appear. At this time, you cannot buy tickets to the movie, though one can imagine that option will be coming very soon.

Finally, Siri, can open apps for you. If you want to open an app, simply say, "Open" and the app's name.

The new iOS lets you add shortcuts to Siri; you can see this in Settings > Siri & Search > Short cuts.

SIRI SHORTCUTS

Siri Shortcuts is one of the most powerful apps on your phone. And probably the one most people never use. What is it?

Shortcuts might not be the best way to describe it. Automation does it more justice, in my opinion. It's a way to teach Siri how to automate the things you do often in life.

Let me give an example:

Let's say you have a playlist when you plug your phone into CarPlay. You always play it on shuffle. You stop it when you get to your location.

The old way of doing this was manually. The new way to do this is just plug in the phone and let your phone do the rest.

Absolutely nothing for you to do.

Siri Shortcuts becomes easier in iOS 13 because it's all built into the phone with a native pre-installed app.

Shortcuts vs. Automation

When you first open the app, you'll see three menus on the bottom: shortcuts, automation, gallery. What's the difference?

Shortcuts are things you can actually add to your phone, sort of like apps—so you could have an icon representing your shortcut right on your Home screen. "Automation" is actions your phone takes when something happens—you plug it into CarPlay, for example, the phone does X. "Gallery" is pre-made automations that you can add.

Using Shortcuts

To create a shortcut, go to the shortcut menu and tap "Create Shortcut."

Next, select: "Add Action."

From here, you define the shortcut. Do you want to have a shortcut whenever you want to play your workout playlist, for example? Tap "Media." I'm going to create a shortcut to call my wife, so I don't have to go into the phone app to do it. Under suggestions, I'm selecting "Call" and "Wife."

The shortcut is created. From here I can tap the '+' button to create an additional action. For example, whenever I call her, get the current driving time so I can tell her how far I am from home.

If I tap the three dots, I can customize the Shortcut.

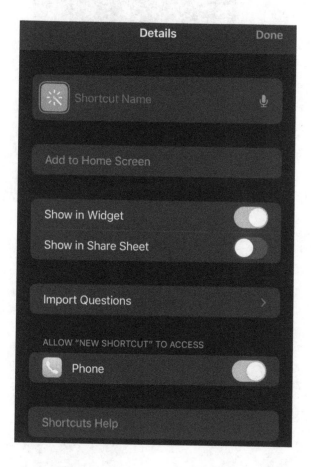

Once I give it a name, I can add it to my Home screen with "Add to Home Screen." From here, if I tap on the small icon, I can choose a custom photo to assign to it.

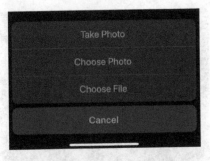

Once you add it, it will appear on your Home screen.

The shortcut also appears in your Siri Shortcut app.

To remove it, long press it. Then tap "Delete."

Using Automation

Adding an automation is similar to the method used for shortcuts. Select "Automation" from the Siri Shortcut menu. You have two options. Personal automation and Home automation. Personal is an automation that would be on your iOS device for you to use. Home automation would be something accessible to anyone in your home and is ideal for something like the Homepod.

Once you select "Create," you'll see a series of suggestions. Select the ones you want and follow the steps.

To remove the automation, swipe over it and select "Delete."

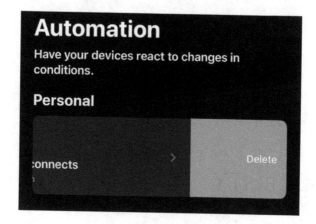

[10]

ACCESSIBILITY

This chapter will cover:
- Vision features
- Interaction features
- Hearing features
- Media & learning features

When it comes to accessibility on the iPhone, there's a lot you can do. To simplify things, I'll break it up into four short sections:
- Vision
- Interaction
- Hearing
- Media & Learning

This will make it easier to skip whatever isn't relevant to you.

Before I get to any of that, where exactly do you find Accessibility? What's great about Apple products is you find things almost the same on any Apple device—which means the way we find accessibility here is the same way you find it on Apple Watch and iPad.

So where is it?!

First, tap the Settings icon.

Next, go to General.

⚙️	General	>

And finally, tap on Accessibility.

Accessibility	>

VISION

Vision accessibility features have more options than any other feature. If you're sitting there thinking, "I can see just fine" I'd still recommend checking out this section. There's more here than just seeing—you may see perfectly fine, but prefer text a little larger or bolder.

VISION	
VoiceOver	Off >
Zoom	Off >
Magnifier	Off >
Display Accommodations	On >
Speech	>
Larger Text	Off >
Bold Text	⬜
Button Shapes	⬜
Reduce Transparency	Off >
Increase Contrast	Off >
Reduce Motion	Off >
On/Off Labels	⬜
Face ID & Attention	>

Below, I'm going to go through the list of accessibility features you should know about, and, if necessary, how to use it. Some will be pretty self-explanatory.

First up: VoiceOver. To access it, just tap VoiceOver.

VoiceOver dictates everything on your screen. What do I mean by "everything"? Exactly that! If you adjust the volume up, then VoiceOver will tell you that the volume has turned up.

To turn this feature on? Flick the toggle. Controlling this feature? Not quite as simple. Turning it on means several of the normal gestures on the iPhone are changed a little.

To go to Home, for example, you swipe up until you feel a vibration; if you want to switch apps, you swipe up a little further until you feel a second vibration.

The voice reading things back is probably a little too fast by default. To slow it down a bit, use the slider under "Speaker Rate." The closer to the turtle icon you get, the slower it will be.

If you like VoiceOver, but don't like how long it takes to read something back, you can make it a little less wordy by tapping on Verbosity.

Braille is an interesting feature on the iPhone. You can't exactly feel braille on your phone, after all. So how does it work? To use it, you need a braille reader that connects to your phone (usually via Bluetooth).

‹ VoiceOver   **Braille**

Output	Eight-dot ›
Input	Six-dot ›
Braille Screen Input	Six-dot ›

Status Cells	›
Equations use Nemeth Code	⬤
Show Onscreen Keyboard	◯
Turn Pages when Panning	⬤
Word Wrap	⬤
Braille Code	English (Unified) ›
Alert Display Duration	3s ›

CHOOSE A BRAILLE DISPLAY...

Searching...

What else about VoiceOver do you need to know? The features under Braille will be a little less commonly used. Rotor controls actions you'll take to receive VoiceOver; Always Speak Notifications toggled on will automatically read back any message you get.

If you decide to use this feature, there's a number of third-party apps that are built for it. Just a few: TapTapSee, Seeing AI, Voice Dream Writer, and Read2Go.

Below VoiceOver is Zoom. Zoom is a bit less intrusive than VoiceOver; it turns on only when you tap the assigned gesture, so you might forget that it's even on.

‹ Accessibility **Zoom**

Zoom

Zoom magnifies the entire screen:
• Double-tap three fingers to zoom
• Drag three fingers to move around the screen
• Double-tap three fingers and drag to change zoom

Follow Focus

Smart Typing

Smart Typing will switch to Window Zoom when a keyboard appears and move the Window so that text is zoomed, but the keyboard is not.

Show Controller

The Zoom Controller allows quick access to zoom controls:
• Tap once to show the Zoom menu
• Double-tap to zoom in and out
• When zoomed in, drag to pan zoom content
• 3D Touch to Peek Zoom

Zoom Region   Full Screen Zoom ›

Zoom Filter   None ›

MAXIMUM ZOOM LEVEL

                                        5.0x

Once you toggle Zoom on, you can activate it at any time by double-tapping with three fingers. Take note here: three fingers! Use one finger and this isn't going to happen—three fingers have to touch the screen. To exit zoom, repeat this.

At the bottom of the screen, there's a slider to adjust the zoom level; by default, it's 5x. You can go up to 15x.

By default, when you tap with three fingers, you'll get a small zoomed in window; want to see the entire screen? Go to Zoom Region, and select Full Screen Zoom.

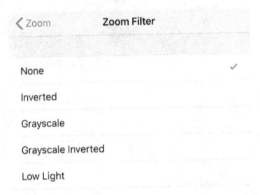

If your phone is in color, but when you zoom, you want it in grey-scale—or any other filter—you can change that in Zoom Filter.

Below Zoom is a handy little feature called "Magnifier."

When you switch the toggle to on, a shortcut is added to use your phone as a magnifying glass. Triple-click the side button and a magnify app opens up.

Near the bottom of the screen is a slider to adjust the zoom.

Display Accommodations is where you can make your screen black and white—or a number of different settings. Just go into Display Accommodations, select Color Filters, toggle Color Filters to on, and select your color scheme.

In Display Accommodations, you can also reduce the intensity of bright colors, turn off auto brightness, and invert colors.

One of the most common accessibility features is Larger Text; when turned on, this increases the font size for all compatible apps. On the bottom of this feature is a slider—adjust it to the right to make the font bigger, and to the left to make it smaller.

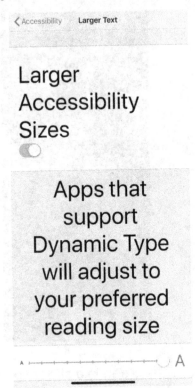

Finally, reduce motion makes the interface a little less—motion-y! What do I mean? The easiest way to explain this is for you to go to your Home screen. Move your phone around. See how the icons and background appear to be moving? If that annoys you or makes you dizzy, then toggle this on.

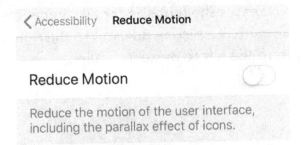

INTERACTION

Interaction is the area that pertains to gestures and the things you touch on the phone to launch different apps and widgets. Some of these require special accessories that do not come with your phone; it will note this when you tap on the feature.

INTERACTION

Reachability	

Swipe down on the bottom edge of the screen to bring the top into reach.

Switch Control	Off >
AssistiveTouch	Off >
Touch Accommodations	Off >
Side Button	>
Siri	>
3D Touch	On >
Tap to Wake	
Keyboard	>
Shake to Undo	On >
Vibration	On >
Call Audio Routing	Automatic >

For the most part, these features will help you if you have difficulty touching the screen and find that you often open or type the wrong things as a result.

The first thing you see in this section is Reachability. This is a very important feature especially if you have the largest iPhone. Have you ever tried to get to those top icons with one hand? If you have large hands, it's doable, but even with large hands, it is a stretch. If you toggle Reachability to on, then you can swipe down on the bottom edge of your screen to bring the rows down.

Swipe back up or tap the top in that greyish area to bring the view back to normal.

AssistiveTouch can use a special accessory, but it doesn't require one. When activated, it becomes a round shape on your screen that works a bit like a large cursor. Tapping it opens up the box below and holding it will close the app. If you really miss that home button on the phone, then you can think of it like a virtual home button—it even looks like one. Tap it once to bring up the menu and hold it to return to the home screen.

The side button is another area some people have difficulty with. This is where you go if you want the side button to respond slower (or quicker).

11:20 ⏎   ⏐⏐⏐ 📶 🔋

‹ Accessibility   **Side Button**

CLICK SPEED

Default   ✓

Slow

Slowest

Adjust the speed required to double or triple-click the
side button.

PRESS AND HOLD TO SPEAK

Siri   ✓

Voice Control

Off

Siri will respond when you press and hold the side button.

Use Passcode for Payments   ⬤

Turn this on to use your passcode to make purchases instead
of double-clicking the side button.

Does Siri never understand you? You aren't alone. I once asked Siri to call my wife and she tried to call John. No idea who John is or how it sounds like "wife"! If you'd rather type to Siri to prevent that kind of mishaps, you can turn it on here.

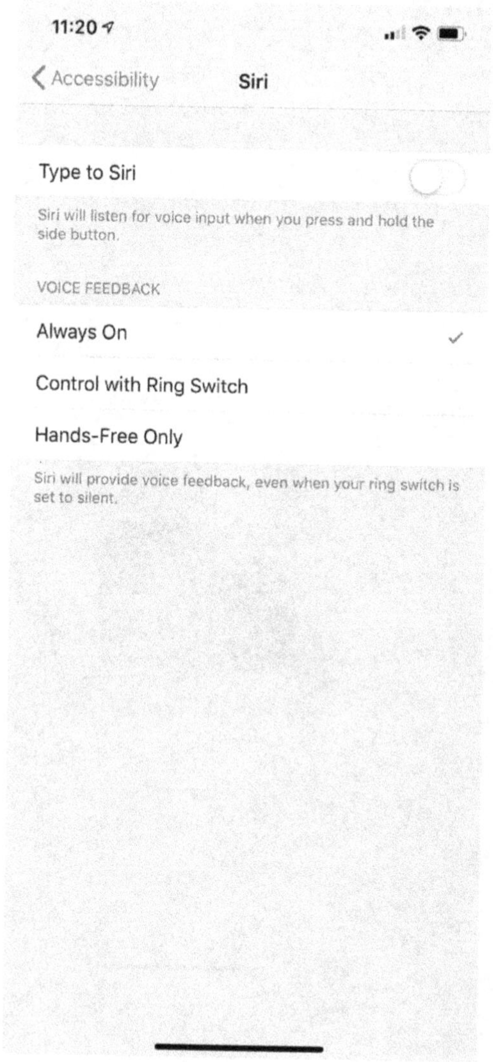

11:20

< Accessibility   **Siri**

Type to Siri

Siri will listen for voice input when you press and hold the side button.

VOICE FEEDBACK

Always On   ✓

Control with Ring Switch

Hands-Free Only

Siri will provide voice feedback, even when your ring switch is set to silent.

3D Touch is how hard you have to push down to activate it. If you find it too difficult to use, then you can adjust the sensitivity here.

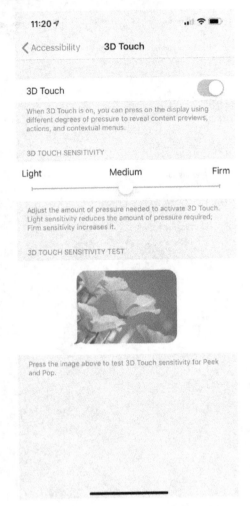

HEARING

If you are using a hearing aid with your phone, then you'll add it and make adjustments to it in this setting. If you are looking for an alternative to a hearing aid, some people use Apple's own AirPods. If you want to do this, then it's recommended that you use third-party apps such as Petralex Hearing Aid. My suggestion, if you want to try this route, is to find cheaper headphones, and see if you even like it before investing in AirPods.

HEARING

MFi Hearing Devices   >

RTT/TTY   Off >

LED Flash for Alerts   Off >

Mono Audio

Phone Noise Cancellation

Noise cancellation reduces ambient noise on phone calls when you are holding the receiver to your ear.

L   R

Adjust the audio volume balance between left and right channels.

Hearing Aid Compatibility

Hearing Aid Compatibility improves audio quality with some hearing aids.

MEDIA & LEARNING

Media and Learning are where you will go to turn on closed captioning for things like movies and TV shows that you purchase, or Audio Descriptions—which means it will read back what is happening in the video.

MEDIA

Subtitles & Captioning   >

Audio Descriptions   Off >

LEARNING

Guided Access   On >

Accessibility Shortcut   Guided Access >

[11]

APPLE SERVICES

This chapter will cover:
- iCloud
- Apple Arcade
- Applte TV+
- Apple News
- Apple Card

It used to be a few times a year Apple would take the stage and announce something that everyone's head exploded over! The iPhone! The iPad! The Apple Watch! The iPod!

That still happens today, but Apple also is well aware of the reality: most people don't upgrade to new hardware every year. How does a company make money when that happens? In a word: services.

In the past few years (especially in 2019) Apple announced several services—things people would opt into to pay for monthly. It was a way to continue making money even when people were not buying hardware.

For it to work, Apple knew it had to be good. They couldn't just offer a subpar service and expect people to pay because it said Apple. It had to be good. And it is!

This book will walk you through those services and show you how to get the most out of them.

ICLOUD

iCloud is something that Apple doesn't talk a lot about but is perhaps their biggest service. It's estimated that nearly 850 million people use it. The thing about it, however, is many people don't even know they're using it.

What exactly is it? If you are familiar with Google Drive, then the concept is something you probably already understand. It's an online storage locker. But it's more than that. It is a place where you can store files, and it also syncs everything—so if you send a message on your iPhone, it appears on your MacBook and iPad. If you work on a Keynote presentation from your iPad, you can continue where you left off on your iPhone.

What's even better about iCloud is it's affordable. New phones get 5GB for free. From there the price range is as follows (note that these prices may change after printing):

- 50GB: $0.99
- 200GB: $2.99
- 2TB: $9.99

These prices are for everyone in your family. So, if you have five people on your plan, then each person doesn't need their own storage plan. This also means purchases are saved—if one family member buys a book or movie, everyone can access it.

iCloud has become even more powerful as our photo library grows. Photos used to be relatively small, but as cameras have advanced, the size goes up. Most photos on your phone are several MB big. iCloud means you can keep the newest ones on your phone and put the older ones in the cloud. It also means you don't have to worry about paying for the phone with the biggest hard drive—in fact, even if you have the biggest hard drive, there's a chance it won't fit all of your photos.

Where Is iCloud?

If you look at your phone, you won't see an iCloud app. That's because there isn't an iCloud app. There's a "Files" app that functions like a storage locker.

To see iCloud, point your computer browser to iCloud.com.

Once you sign in, you'll see all the things stored in your cloud—photos, contacts, notes, files; these are all things you can access across all of your devices.

In addition, you can use iCloud from any computer (even PCs); this is especially helpful if you need to use Find iPhone, which locates not only your iPhone, but all of your Apple devices—phones, watches, even AirPods.

Backing Up Your Phone With iCloud

The first thing you should know about iCloud is how to back up your phone with it. This is what you will need to do if you are moving from one phone to another.

If there's no iCloud app on the phone, then how do you do that? While there is no native app in the traditional sense that you are used to, there are several iCloud settings in the Settings app.

Open the Settings app; at the top you will see your name and profile picture; tap that.

This opens my ID settings where I can update things like phone numbers and email. One of the options is iCloud. Tap that.

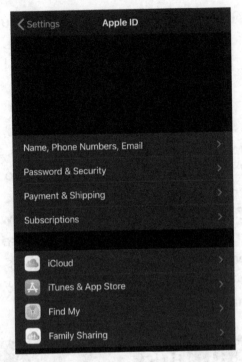

Scroll down a little until you get to the setting that says iCloud Backup, and tap that.

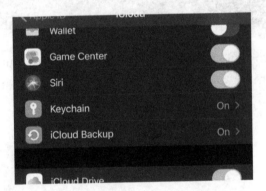

It will probably be on (the toggle switch will be green); if you'd rather do things manually, then you can toggle it off and then do Back Up Now. If you turn it off then you'll have to do a manual backup each time.

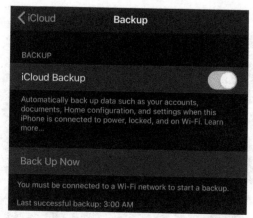

From the iCloud, you'll also be able to change what apps use iCloud and see how much space you have left. In my case, I have the 2TB plan, and we've used about half of it.

If you tap Manage Storage, you can see where the storage is being used. You can also upgrade or downgrade your account from this page by tapping on Change Storage Plan.

Tap on Family Usage and you can see more specifically what family members use what. You can also stop sharing from this page.

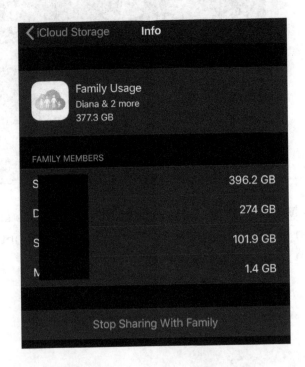

Moving to a New Device

When you get a new device, you will be asked during the setup to log in with your Apple ID associated with your previous device, and then get the option to recover from a previous device.

Sharing Photos With iCloud

To share and backup photos with iCloud, go into Settings > Photos and ensure iCloud Photos is toggled to green. If you are short on storage, you can check the option below to Optimize storage.

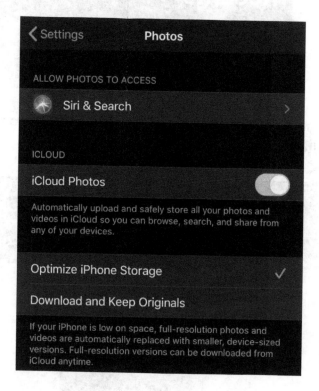

Files App

To see your cloud files, open the Files app.

The first thing you'll see is all your recent files.

If you don't see what you are looking for, then go to the bottom tabs and switch from Recents to Browse.

This opens a more traditional looking file explorer.

If you want to create a new folder, connect to a server, or scan a document, tap the three dots in the top left corner to open your app options.

Scan Documents lets you use your camera like a traditional flatbed scanner to scan and print documents.

You can tap on Sort by Name to change how files are sorted.

iCloud Settings

One other important set of iCloud settings is in Settings > General > iPhone Storage.

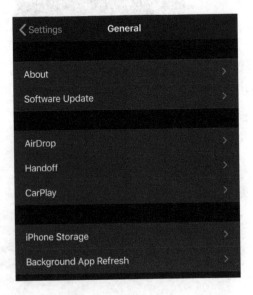

When you tap this, it will show you how much storage apps are using and also make recommendations.

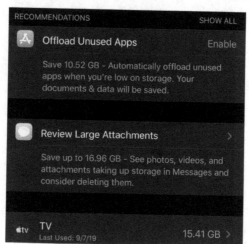

APPLE ARCADE

Apple Arcade is sort of like Netflix for games. It's $4.99/month (nothing extra for other members of your family—share it with up to five members).

The price gives you access to 100+ games. Unlike some streaming services where you have to play the games online, Apple Arcade lets you download the games to play them offline. You can play them on all your Apple compatible devices: iPhone, iPad, and Apple TV. When you stop playing on your phone, you can start playing where you left off on your TV or iPad.

There are no ads and you can use it with parental controls.

How to Sign Up

Apple Arcade isn't an app. It's a Service. You only download what you want. You sign up by visiting the app store and tapping on Arcade. This brings you to the main Arcade menu where all you have to do is tap Subscribe.

Once you subscribe, you'll see a welcome menu.

The Arcade menu is now replaced by games you can download. Tap "Get" for any game you want. $4.99 is for everything—not per app.

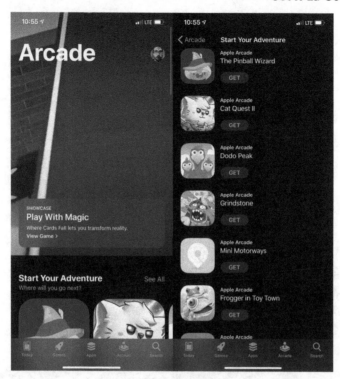

When you read about the game, be mindful of the app size; if you have data restrictions, make sure you download it over Wi-Fi.

The app looks like every other app on your phone. The only difference is the splash screen, which says "Arcade."

Cancelling Arcade Subscription

All subscriptions are cancelled the same way. Go to the app store, and tap your account. Next, tap Subscriptions.

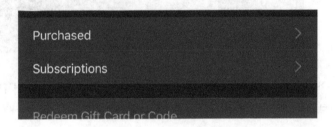

This shows you all of your active subscriptions, including Apple Arcade.

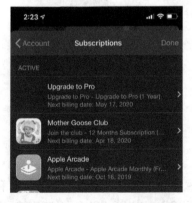

Once you click on it, there is an option to cancel on the bottom.

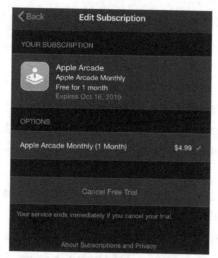

You will get a notification that all of your games will be erased after your subscription expiration (note: it expires on the original expiration date—not the date you cancel).

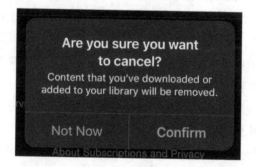

The subscription details now tells you when it's cancelled.

APPLE TV+

Apple has been quietly working on a TV service for quite some time. In 2019, they finally revealed the details. It will be $4.99 a month (free for a year if you buy an iPhone, iPad, Apple Watch, Apple TV, or Mac—note that this may change in the future). It will be available on November 1.

At this printing, there are still some unknowns—notably when certain shows will be released and how many there will be when it launches. What Apple has said is they are trying to be like Netflix, having thousands of things to watch. They are focused on quality over quantity.

The shows that are planned to be released on November 1 (again, this could change after this printing):

- The Morning Show – A show about the drama behind the scenes of a morning TV show; it stars Jennifer Aniston, Reese Witherspoon, and Steve Carell.
- Dickinson – A period piece (with a modern flair) about the poet Emily Dickinson starring Haley Steinfeld.
- For All Mankind – An alternative reality drama that imagines what would have happened if the space race had never ended.
- See – An apocalyptic drama starring Jason Momoa about humans trying to survive in a world where nobody can see.
- The Elephant Queen – A documentary about the threat of elephant extinction.
- Snoopy In Space – A new series from Peanuts (i.e. Charlie Brown and company).
- Helpsters – A kids series from the creators of Sesame Street.
- Ghostwriter – A new twist to a 90s kids TV show.

More shows may be out in November, and more shows will definitely come each month—Apple plans to have at least one show/movie out a month. Apple has announced (with no set release dates) that it plans to work with such directors as J. J. Abrams, Steven Spielberg, and M. Night Shyamalan, and actors like Octavia Spencer, Brie Larson, and Jennifer Garner. A new Oprah Winfrey show will also be released.

You'll be able to, of course, watch these shows on Apple TV, iPhone, and iPads.

APPLE MUSIC

Apple Music is Apple's music streaming service.

The question most people wonder is which is better: Spotify or Apple Music? On paper it's hard to tell. They both have the same number of songs, and they both cost the same ($9.99 a month, $5 for students, $14.99 for families).

There really is no clear winner. It all comes down to preference. Spotify has some good features—such as an ad-supported free plan.

One of the standout features of Apple Music is iTunes Match. If you are like me and have a large collection of audio files on your computer, then you'll love iTunes Match. Apple puts those files in the cloud, and you can stream them on any of your devices. This feature is also available if you don't have Apple Music for $25 a year.

Apple Music also plays well with Apple devices; so, if you are an Apple house (i.e. everything you own, from smart speakers to TV media boxes, has the Apple logo), then Apple Music is probably the best one for you.

Apple is compatible with other smart speakers, but it's built to shine on its own devices.

I won't cover Spotify here, but my advice is to try them both (they both have free trials) and see which interface you prefer.

Apple Music Crash Course

Before going over where things are in Apple Music, it's worth noting that Apple Music can now be accessed from your web browser (in beta form) here: http://beta.music.apple.com.

It's also worth noting that I have a little girl and don't get to listen to a lot of "adult" music, so the examples here are going to show a lot of kids music!

The main navigation on Apple Music is at the bottom. There are five basic menus to select from:

- Library
- For You
- Browse
- Radio
- Search

Library

When you create playlists or download songs or albums, this is where you will go to find them.

You can change the categories that show up in this first list by tapping on Edit, then checking off the categories you want. Make sure to hit Done to save your changes.

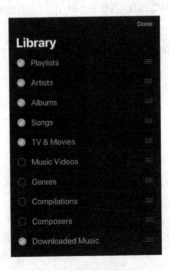

When you tap on the playlist you want to play, you can also share it with your friends by tapping on the three dots that show the options menu, and then tapping on Share Playlist.

For You

As you play music, Apple Music starts to get to know you more and more; it makes recommendations based on what you are playing. In For You, you can get a mix of all these songs and see other recommendations.

In addition to different styles of music, it also has friends' recommendations so you can discover new music based on what your friends are listening to.

Browse

Not digging those recommendations? You can also browse genres in the Browse menu. In addition to different genre categories, you can see what music is new and what music is popular.

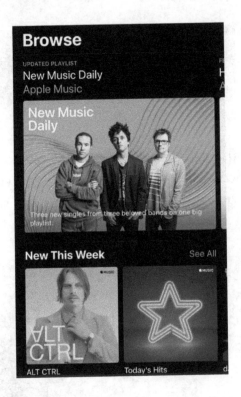

Radio

Radio is Apple's version of AM/FM; the main radio station is Beats One. There are on-air DJs and everything you'd expect from a radio station.

While Beats One is Apple's flagship station, it's not its only station. You can scroll down and tap on Radio Stations under More to explore and see several other stations based on music styles (i.e. country, alternative, rock, etc.). Under this menu, you'll also find a handful of talk stations covering news and sports. Don't expect to find the opinionated talk radio you may listen to on regular radio—it's pretty controversy-free.

Search

The last option is the search menu, which is pretty self-explanatory. Type in what you want to find (i.e. artist, album, genre, etc.).

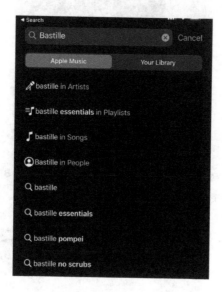

Listening to Music and Creating a Playlist

You can access the music you are currently listening to from the bottom of your screen.

This brings up a full screen of what you are listening to with several options.

The play, back/forward, and volume buttons are pretty straightforward. The buttons below that might look new.

The first option is for lyrics. If the song is paused, then you can read through the lyrics; if the song is playing, then it will bold the lyrics to the song it is currently playing. If you ever caught yourself wondering if the singer is saying "dense" or "dance" then this feature is a game-changer.

The middle option lets you pick where you play the music. For example, if you have a HomePod and you want to listen wirelessly to the music from that device, you can change it here.

The last option shows the next song(s) in the playlist.

If you want to add a song to a playlist, then click the three dots next to the album/artist name. This brings up a list of several options (you can also go here to love or hate a song—which helps Apple Music figure out what you like); the option you want is Add to a Playlist. If you don't have a playlist or want to add it to a new one, then you can also create one here.

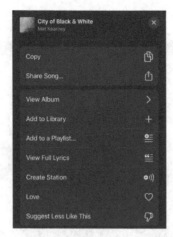

At any point, you can tap the artist's name to see all of their music.

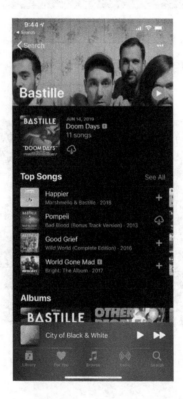

In addition to seeing information about the band, their popular songs, and their albums, you can get a playlist of their essential songs or a playlist of bands that they have influenced.

If you scroll to the bottom, you can also see Similar Artists, which is a great way to discover new bands that are like the ones you are currently listening to.

Tips for Getting the Most Out of Apple Music

Heart It

Like what your hearing? Heart it! Hate it? Dislike it. Apple gets to know you by what you listen to, but it improves the accuracy when you tell it what you think of a song you are really into...or really hate.

Use Settings

Some of the most resourceful features of Apple Music aren't in Apple Music—they're in your settings.

Open the Settings app, and scroll down to Music.

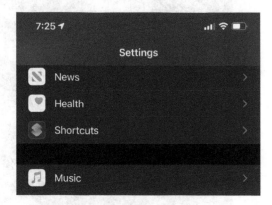

There are a few things to note here.

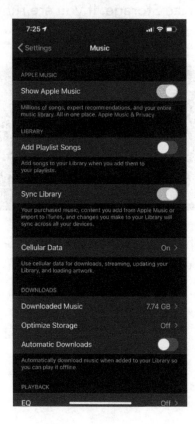

The first is under Cellular Data. Tap that and you'll see an option to turn high quality streaming on and off. If you want the best quality even when you are using data, then turn it on.

Next, go to Optimize Storage. If you are running short on space, then make sure and tap to toggle off.

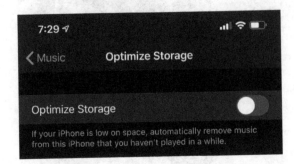

Want to change the way your music sounds—such as more or less bass—go to EQ in the settings.

Download Music

If you don't want to rely on data when you are on the go, make sure and tap the Cloud on your music to download the music locally to your phone. If you don't see a cloud, add it to your library by tapping the plus, which should change it to a cloud.

Hey Siri

Siri knows music! Say "Hey Siri" and say what you want to listen to, and the AI will get to work.

Wake Up to Music

If you'd like to wake up to a song instead of a buzzing noise, open your alarm. Next, tap "Sound."

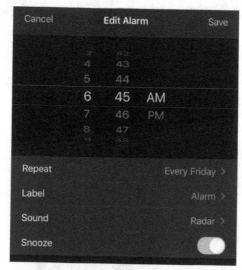

From here, select "Pick a Song."

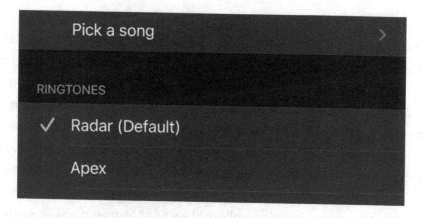

Finally, pick your music.

APPLE NEWS+

In 2012, a little app with big ambitions called Next (it was later changed to Texture) disrupted the magazine industry by creating the Netflix of magazines. For one low price, you could read hundreds of magazines (and their back issues too). They weren't small indie magazines—they were the big ones: People, Time, Wired, and more.

Apple took notice, and, in 2018, they acquired the company. The writing was on the wall: Apple wanted to get into print services.

In 2019, it was announced that Texture would close because Apple would release a new service called News+. News+ does everything that Texture did, but also combines newspapers (Los Angeles Times and The Wall Street Journal).

There is a free version of the service that curates news for you; the paid version that carries the magazine subscriptions is $9.99. (You can have five family members on your plan.)

What really makes Apple News stand out is it's curated for you and your tastes. If you have other family members on your plan, it will be curated for them as well—it's based on the user's tastes, so if you have a family member into entertainment news and you are into game news, you won't see their interests—only yours.

Apple News Crash Course

To get started, open the News app from your phone (if it is not on your phone, it's a free download from the app store)

The UI for the app is pretty simple. There are three menu options on the bottom:

Today–This is where you'll find your curated news

News+—Where you'll find magazines

Following—This is where you can change your interests and un-follow certain news.

Today

The Today menu gives you all your news (starting with the top news/breaking news) in a scrolling format.

The app relies a lot on gestures. Swipe left over a headline/story and you'll get options to suggest more stories like it, share the story, or save the story for later.

Swipe right over a story, and you can dislike it (so it stops showing similar stories) or report it. Typically, "report" in a news app means you find it somehow inappropriate in nature; that's true here, but there are other reasons to report it—such as, it's dated wrong, it's in the wrong category, it's a broken link, or something else.

As you scroll down, you start seeing different categories (Trending Stories in the example below); when you tap the three dots with a circle, you'll get an option to block it so it won't show in your feed any longer.

When you tap to read a story, there are only a few options. At the top, there's the option to make the text larger or smaller; next to that is the option to share the story with friends (assuming they have Apple News). To get to the next story, there's an option in the lower right corner (or swipe left from the right corner of the screen); to get back to the previous page, tap the back arrow in the upper left corner or swipe right from the left side of the screen.

One criticism of Apple News by some has been its UI; when Apple announced the service along with its partnership with the Los Angeles Times and Wall Street Journal, many expected a format similar to what you have seen with the magazines section—a full newspaper type layout.

Worse, many didn't even know how to find the newspaper. And if they did find it, they couldn't search for stories. While the app is pretty resourceful, this is still an early product and some of the features you want might not be there yet.

That said, you can "kind of" read the Los Angeles Times (or any newspaper in Apple News) in a more traditional way. First, find an article in your feed from the publication you want to see more from, and then click the publication's name at the top of the story.

Los Angeles Times

This will bring up the publication along with all the topics from that publication.

If you want to search for a particular story or publication, then head over to Following on the tab at the bottom of the screen, and search for what you want to find.

Following

Since we are on the Following tab, let's talk about it for a minute, and then go back to the middle tab (News+).

This is where you are going to be able to look at your history, read saved stories (as noted above), search for stories and publications, and follow or unfollow topics.

To unfollow a category, swipe left over it and select unfollow.

To add a new category, scroll down a little. You'll see suggested topics. Tap the + for any you want to follow.

You can move your categories around by tapping on the Edit button at the top right.

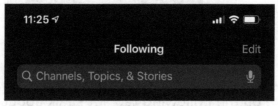

News+

The last section to cover is News+; this is where you'll find all the magazines you love.

The format is similar to the Today screen; magazines you read are at the top; below that are stories pulled from several different magazines that the app thinks you'll be interested in. There's also a more personalized For You section.

When you read articles from the list, it opens in the actual magazine and looks a little different from articles in the Today area.

Anytime you want to read more from a magazine (or see back issues) just click the logo from an article you are reading.

That brings up a list of all the issues you can read as well as some of the latest stories from the magazine.

Tapping the + button in the upper right corner will let you follow the publication.

If you long press (press and hold) the magazine cover from your My Magazines section, you can also unfollow, delete, or see back issues from the publication.

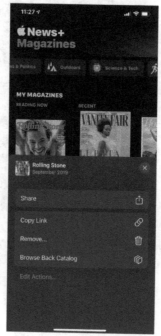

To browse all the magazines available, select Browse the Catalog from the main screen (or browse by a category that you are interested in).

This brings up a list of all the magazines you can read (at this writing, there are around 300).

Long press any of them and you can download the magazine, follow it, block it, or browse the back-issue library.

Apple Card

One of Apple's most talked about new products is Apple Card. Apple Card is a credit card that, at first glance, doesn't differ from most credit cards. It may not have the best rewards (1% to 3% cash back depending on your purchase) or best interest rate, but that doesn't mean it's not disrupting the industry; it's definitely something you should consider getting.

On the surface, the advantage of Apple Card is receiving your rewards the next day—not waiting for them. That's nice. But where it excels is in security and how it helps you keep track of purchases.

Getting Your Card

Getting an Apple Card will probably be the easiest credit card sign up you have ever experienced in your life. To get started, go to the Wallet app on your iPhone.

When the app opens, click the + button and follow the application. It will just ask you a series of questions and then tell you if you are approved.

If you're approved, your card will appear in your Wallet app with other cards.

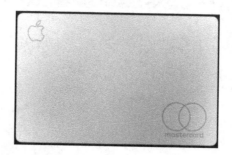

When There Is No Apple Pay

Once you are approved for the card, you can start using it! There's no need to wait for the card—in fact the rewards are better if you don't use the card!

But sometimes you need a card. Not everyone accepts Apple Pay, after all. Fortunately, you can request a card.

You'll probably be surprised by the card. It's thick. Like really thick. Like probably the thickest card in your wallet! You can't even bend it. It doesn't feel like a plastic card. It feels like metal. That's because it's made of metal. It's not heavy at all, fortunately.

It takes about a week to arrive, and activating it is probably going to impress you. There's no number to call. No number to input on a website. None of that stuff.

It comes in a stylish envelope; when you lift the flap of the envelope and put it next to the bottom of your iPhone, it will recognize the card and start the activation process. It looks a bit like the screen below— the card in the illustration was already activated, so the steps no longer are there. The whole process is quick, stylish, and seamless—everything you'd expect from Apple.

Many people think they have to wait for their card to use it online where Apple Pay isn't accepted. That's not true. You just need the credit card number. I know, I know—there is no credit card number! That's where you are wrong. There's no visible number, but there is a number.

To see it, tap the card in your Wallet app, and then tap the three little dots near the top.

This opens up your account information where you can see your credit limit, interest rate, make payments, and contact support. One of the options is "Card Information."

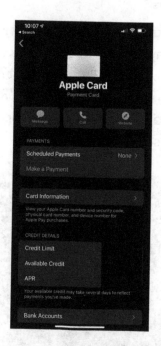

Here you'll be able to see your card number, expiration, and security card. Worried someone has your number? Just request a new number.

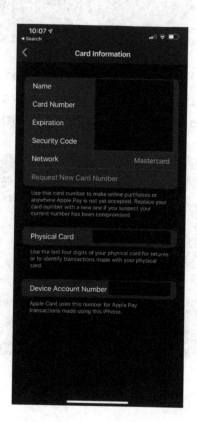

Requesting a new number doesn't affect your physical card. If someone steals your physical card, then make sure you deactivate that, and request a new card. How do you do that? Hit the back arrow to go back to your account menu. Scroll down to "Request Replacement Card." This will suspend your account to stop any future transactions and a new card will be sent.

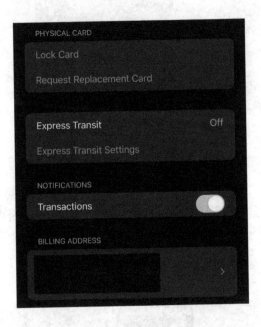

What if you want to remove the card? Go back a screen, and then go to the bottom of the screen and tap Remove This Card (remember, however, that this won't close out your account).

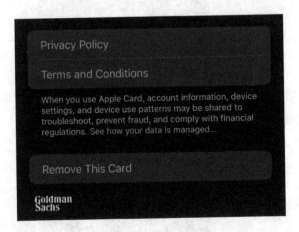

Seeing Card Activity

When you tap your card from the Wallet app, you can see all your activity, such as balance, when the payment is due, and recent transactions.

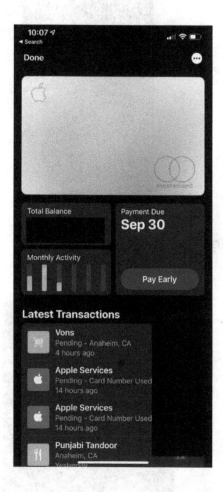

Not sure what a transaction is? Tap on it and you'll get more information about the store, and, in many cases, see a map of where it was purchased. This is helpful when tracking down mystery payments, which appear on other credit cards with weird names that don't make any sense and seem more like codes than businesses.

If you tap on Monthly Activity from the previous screen, you can see the categories in which you are spending money. You can also see your rewards.

The big question on your mind might be how you spend those rewards. The rewards money is on a separate card called a Cash Card that you can access from your Wallet app. You can spend the money by using it anywhere that takes Apple Pay, or you can transfer the money straight to your bank account. You can also use the Cash Card to text money to friends.

Making Payments and Seeing Statements

To make a payment to your card, go to your main card page and tap the Payment Due box. This brings up your payment information. Interest is very transparent on Apple Card. See those dots on the circle? Tap the check mark and drag it to one of those dots; this tells you what your interest charge would be by only making a portion of the payment. Drag to the area you want to pay and then select Pay Now (or Pay Later to schedule the payment). If you don't have your bank account set up, then you'll have to do that at this point—you'll need your bank account number and routing information.

To see your credit card statement, tap Total Balance from the main menu. Go to the bottom and select the statement you want to see.

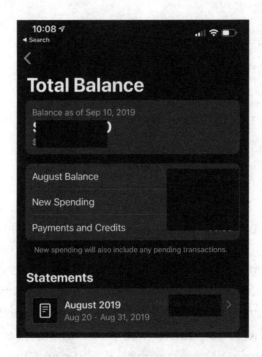

This brings up a brief, high-level, digital statement.

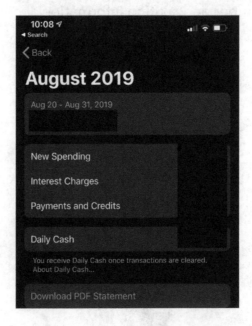

If you want to see your full statement—the long paper one you'd typically get in the mail from other credit cards—then tap Download PDF Statement.

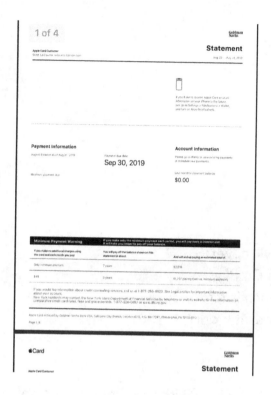

[12]

CARPLAY

This chapter will cover:
- What is CarPlay
- How much is it?
- How does it work?

CarPlay doesn't come with the iPhone—the software is there, but the actual hardware is extra. So why include it here? Because it's becoming more common in new cars.

WHAT IS CARPLAY

In 2014, Apple announced something called CarPlay. At the time it wasn't met with much fanfare because to play it, you needed a radio in your car that most people didn't have. Today, many newer cars have it pre-installed; if you aren't one of the lucky ones, you can buy a compatible radio with CarPlay for less than $200—before installation.

So what is it? Think of it like an external screen for your car—plug your phone in and it "sort of" mirrors your iPhone to your car radio. I say "sort of" because it doesn't quite look like your phone—it's a car friendly version of your phone. For example, when you tap your messages on your phone, you don't see your messages, you hear them—as in it reads your messages to you. The goal of CarPlay is to give you a more distraction-free experience so you can safely use your phone while driving. Siri is a big part of CarPlay, which means it can be voice controlled and your hands can stay on the wheel.

The good thing about CarPlay is you don't have to buy any extra new software—it's already built into your phone even if you don't have a CarPlay device. Once you plug it into the car radio you are done. No complicated setup. No setup at all! It just works. When your phone updates, it updates CarPlay as well. There's nothing extra to do. As soon as you plug it in, then the new OS is there.

Your old radio is still there; CarPlay is just like an app that runs on top of it. The below example shows you my main radio home screen. To jump back to CarPlay, I just press the CarPlay button.

It's free to use, although a few cars charge a service fee. If you buy your own radio, however, there will be no extra fees.

How Much?

As I mentioned, it's free to use—but you still need a radio (although the car manufacture could technically charge fees). CarPlay radios cost less than $200 online and go all the way up to over $1,000—these higher priced radios usually have wireless connections so you don't even have to plug your phone in.

If your car doesn't have it and you decide to install it, there are a few things to keep in mind:

Installation fees. A lot of places will advertise a free installation. That's technically true—they'll install the radio for free, but then to get it to work in your car, they'll tell you about special adaptors and mounts that you need, which are not free to install. Depending on your car, you probably will spend $400 to $600 to have a CarPlay unit installed in your car.

Adaptors. Be mindful of what adaptors you need. Have a backup camera? You'll probably need a separate adaptor. Have Sirius radio? Another adaptor. Want to control your radio from your steering wheel? Another adaptor! There are often a lot of extra fees.

Understand the adapters. My car has the ability to control the radio from the steering wheel. When my radio broke and I bought a CarPlay unit, I didn't bother with the adaptor. It's not that hard to reach over and control the radio after all! But because there were other buttons on the steering wheel, it disconnected everything. A few weeks later, my maintenance light came on. I fixed it but the light wouldn't turn off because the mechanic needed the steering wheel button to reset it. So, it was back to the radio shop to have another adapter added to the radio!

Can you install it yourself? Definitely! But this is not a newbie project. The radio itself is pretty simple, but newer cars don't make it easy to get radios out. You often need special tools. You also will probably be spending a lot of time looking for YouTube videos on the topic. It's not impossible, but do your research before deciding you are going to do it yourself and not just pay someone to do it for you.

Is it worth it? It's a lot of money up front, but it's also a much better radio experience. My old radio had a hard time with Bluetooth, and half the time it wouldn't connect to my phone. Not to mention, it was hard to get directions on the built-in map without pulling over and spending ten minutes trying to type the address in. The CarPlay radio really does provide a more handsfree experience and keeps my eyes on the road and never on the phone. So, for me it was worth the price.

How Does CarPlay Work?

Think of CarPlay a little like an AppleTV plugged into your TV. Your TV is not an AppleTV; your TV is just showing what's on the AppleTV. If you leave it on, but change to a different TV input, the AppleTV is still on. That's basically CarPlay.

Once you plug your phone into the lightning cable adaptor that's connected to your radio, your phone will show a CarPlay screen.

Meanwhile, your radio will automatically launch CarPlay OS.

The whole process takes just a few seconds. At any point, you can go back to your car radio while still running CarPlay—it's a bit like switching inputs on a TV. Most CarPlay compatible radios have a button that toggles between the two.

Here's something else most CarPlay radios have: Android Auto.

Android Auto is the Android equivalent of CarPlay; so if you happen to have an Android device as well, then you'll be able to run both—one at a time.

When you launch CarPlay, you might be a little surprised that it only has a few apps—only a small fraction of the apps on your phone appear there. That's because the only apps that run in CarPlay are apps that are appropriate for the car.

The interface is very simple. The bottom indicates how many screens you have with apps (two in my case); swipe left and right to toggle between them. Tap any icon to launch the app.

To the left is the main menu for CarPlay. In the upper left corner is the time and data network connection (it's using your phone's data); below that are the three most recent apps you have open; tapping once will launch them; tapping the bottom left corner will either hide the current app or put it into a split, three-pane view (that means it will show your map and minimized versions of two other apps—Apple Music and Apple Calendar, for example).

Here's an example of a three-pane view; notice how the button in the lower, left corner changed; that means if you tap it again, it will show all apps.

HOW APPS WORK

What do the actual apps look like in CarPlay? Some are nicer than others; I'll walk you through the main ones next. As you can expect, all the apps are pretty minimalistic and keep you from doing too many actions—because your eyes need to be on the road!

At any time, you can say "Hey Siri" and activate voice commands on CarPlay. You can tell it to find music, text someone, get directions, and more—it works the same way as your phone except there's no need to unlock anything to activate the app.

Maps

The star of CarPlay is Maps. To access it, just click the Map app from the main screen.

This will launch a full-screen version of the app.

On the right side are a couple of controls you probably won't use often.

The arrow pinpoints where you currently are—so if you are searching for something several miles away, this would bring the map to your current location. The 3-D option just changes the angle of the map.

The + / - zoom in and out of the map.

On the left side is an option to search or find saved destinations. Remember, at any time you can say "Hey Siri" and give voice commands. For example, "Hey Siri, find me the closest gas station."

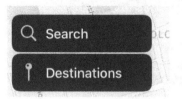

When you tap Search, it will give you suggested categories, a mic to dictate what you want to find, or a keyboard to type it out on the onscreen keyboard.

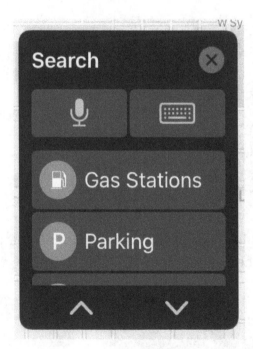

When the results come up, it will pinpoint them on the screen so you can decide which one you want to go to.

When you find the one you want, just tap on it. You'll be shown a suggested direction, and you can either call the location or tap Go to get the directions.

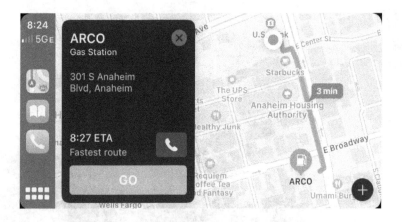

As you drive, it will have the turn-by-turn navigation in the upper left corner and the estimated arrival time in the lower left corner.

If you tap the up arrow in the lower left corner, it will bring up driving options. They're all self-explanatory. The one I find most helpful is "Share ETA."

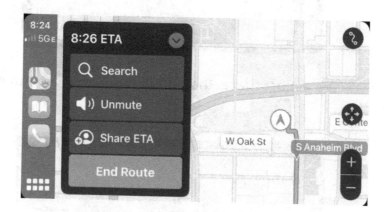

Share ETA lets you send your current location to a person so they can keep track of when you'll arrive and if you'll be late. To share the ETA, just tap the person's name.

Once you start sharing, that person is sent a text message that looks like the one below:

When you are almost there, they get another message that looks like this:

If you are running more than a few minutes late, they'll get a text with an updated time.

At any time, you can press the button in the lower left corner to get the three-pane view of the map.

If you look at your phone with your map on, then you'll see the turn-by-turn directions.

Google Maps

I am not going to cover third-party apps at any length, but to give you a quick look at what another map app looks like on CarPlay, the below quickly walks you through Google Maps.

Open the app and you'll be greeted with a similar simplicity. One noticeable distinction is the settings icon in the upper right corner.

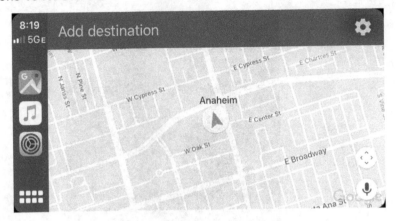

Tapping on the settings icon takes you to a settings menu where you can configure the app.

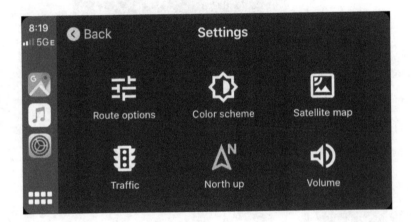

Unlike Apple Maps, Google Maps has satellite imagery in CarPlay, which may or may not be important to you.

When you tap Destinations, you get a screen that's not too different from Apple Maps (albeit larger), and you can search for things by category.

Tap on those categories and you'll get a list of locations.

Once you make your selection, tapping Go will start the turn-by-turn navigation.

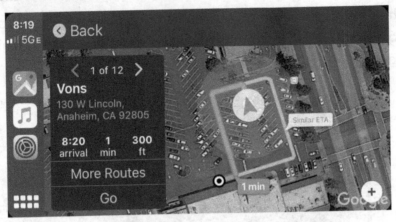

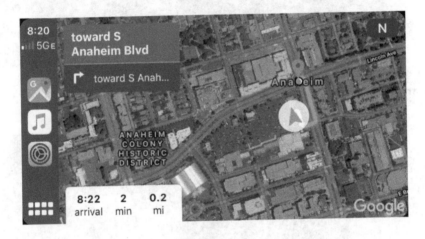

Apple Music

Apple has taken great strives to create a music app, and, not surprisingly, the Music app is one of the standout features of CarPlay. Tap the music icon to launch it.

The reason it stands out on CarPlay is not so much all the features it has, rather the features it doesn't have. It's simple and lets you quickly navigate, which is what you want while you are driving.

This is not a place to manage all your music—you do that on your phone. This is a place to listen to what you've already organized.

When you open the app, you'll notice a menu on the top with five options.

The library shows all the albums you have added.

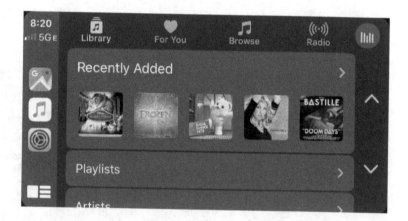

For You shows you suggestions based on what you've been listing to.

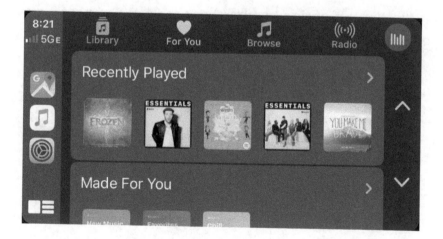

Browse lets you look at different genres of music—or play what's popular.

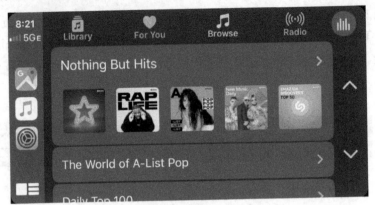

Radio is a combination of playlists that are created by Apple and playlists based on what you are listening to.

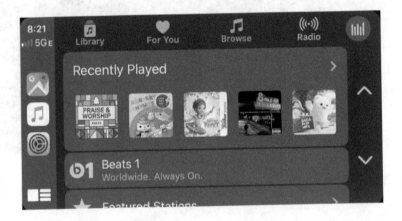

Finally, the last option (the bars) opens what's currently playing.

Calendar

The calendar app is pretty simple.

It shows your upcoming events.

Settings

Settings on the iPhone is very large. On CarPlay? Not so much.

There's just a handful of options, and most of them are just toggles. If you haven't noticed, the goal of CarPlay is minimal touching, so your eyes are on the road and not the screen.

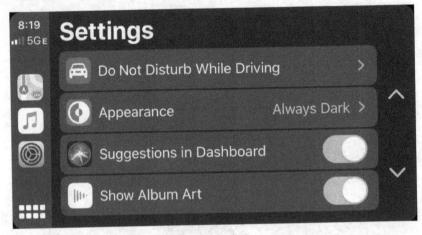

Do Not Disturb While Driving turns off most features, but you can still use music and maps.

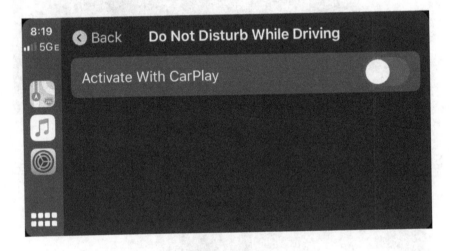

Phone

Making calls through CarPlay can be done by asking Siri or tapping on the phone app.

Like the Music app, the Phone app has a very simple top navigation menu. These menus are all configured on your phone—which means you don't use CarPlay to add a contact, you use your phone.

Favorites is where you put the people you call most. Mine only has one, and, again, this is configured on my phone.

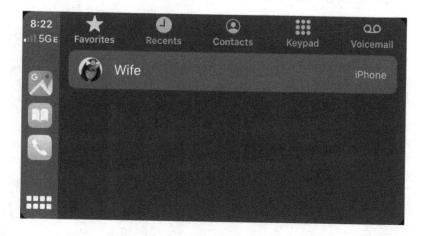

Recents is a list of who has called you or who you have called.

Contacts is a list of all the people in your contacts app. Because this list is usually pretty long, there's an option to activate Siri at the top. Or you can just say "Hey Siri."

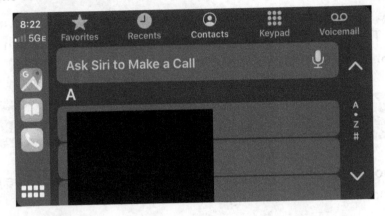

Keypad lets you dial the old fashion way.

Voicemail shows a list of all your current voicemail.

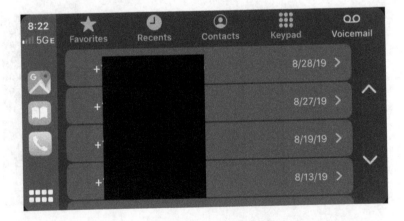

Tapping on any of them will let you listen to the recording.

Messaging
The messaging app might not be what you think.

If you are thinking an onscreen keyboard, then you are wrong. That would be too much of a distraction. Messages shows you a list of your messages. Tap it and it disctates the message back to you—there is no option to read the message, because, again, your eyes should be on the road!

The only option here besides listening to a message is to compose a new one—that option is in the upper right corner. You don't compose a message like you do on a phone with a keyboard—you dictate it.

Audiobooks

If you have purchased audiobooks from Apple Books, then they'll be here.

It's a very simple app—just a list of the audiobooks that you own.

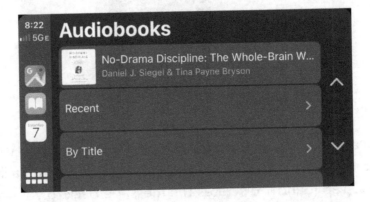

Podcasts

Podcasts is similar to the Music app, but with less options.

The top menu has three different tabs.

Listen Now has all the Podcast episodes you have queued to play. The cloud indicates that it hasn't been downloaded, so you will be streaming it.

Library lists the shows you follow; tap them to see individual episodes.

Browse lets you look for new Podcasts.

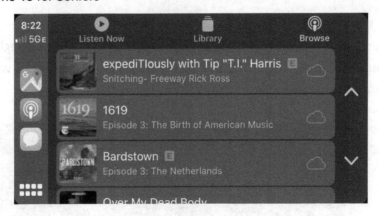

Screenshots

Not an app, but a pretty cool little feature is the screenshot tool. Normally when you do a screenshot on your phone (you do this by pressing the side button and volume down button at the same time) it takes a screenshot of your phone.

When your phone is plugged into your radio, it takes two screen-shots: one of your phone's screen and one of your CarPlay Screen.

OTHER APPS

It shouldn't be a surprise that most of the apps you see on CarPlay are Apple apps. Because driving is involved, this is not a place for game apps or video apps. App developers do have CarPlay apps, but there aren't many. Most are music and map related. Below are some of the most popular apps:

- Waze – a map app that relies heavily on users reporting traffic problems; it's one of the most popular driving apps, and is known for finding alternative routes to get you to your destination at the quickest possible time based on traffic data.
- TomTom – another map app; one of the features this one is known for is showing the lane you need to be in. It's helpful if you are on the freeway and don't know what lanes merge onto what freeways.
- TuneIn – Known for one of the largest collections of streaming content; it has lots of radio shows, podcasts, and sports.
- iHeartRadio – Find radio stations from around the world with this popular app.
- Audible – Apple has an audiobook app in CarPlay, but it doesn't hold up against Audible, which is owned by Amazon and has one of the largest audiobook collections available for a small monthly subscription.
- Free Audiobooks – Not a fan of subscriptions or paying for books? This app has lots of free audio books.
- NPR – The national broadcasting company has all their popular radio shows on this app.
- MLB at Bat – If you are a fan of the videos in the iPhone app, then be disappointed. It's not supported here. But there is audio commentary and more.
- Spotify – Apple Music's biggest streaming competitor.
- Pandora – A music app based on what you like; you can't just tell it to play the song you want to hear, but you can tell it to play songs like it.

[13]

MAINTAIN AND PROTECT

This chapter will cover:
- Security
- Encryption
- Keychain
- Battery tips

SECURITY

Passcode (dos and don'ts, tips, etc.)

In this day and age, it's important to keep your device secure. You may or may not want to set up a Touch ID (you will read more about it next), but at the very least it's a good idea to maintain a passcode. Anytime your phone is unlocked, restarted, updated, or erased, it will require a passcode before allowing entry into the phone. To set up a passcode for your iPhone, go to Settings > Passcode, and click on "Turn Passcode On." You will be prompted to enter a passcode, then re-enter to confirm. Here are a few tips to follow for maximum security:

Do's

DO create a unique passcode that only you would know

DO change it every now and then to keep it unknown

DO select a passcode that can be easily modified later when it's time to change passcodes

Don'ts

DON'T use a simple passcode like 1234 or 5678

DON'T use your birthday or birth year

DON'T use a passcode someone else might have (for example, a shared debit card pin)

DON'T go right down the middle (2580) or sides (1470 or 3690)

ENCRYPTION

With all of the personal and sensitive information that can be stored on iCloud, security is understandably a very real concern. Apple agrees with this and protects your data with high level 128-bit AES encryption. Keychain, which you will learn about next, uses 256-bit AES encryption—the same level of encryption used by all of the top banks who need high levels of security for their data. According to Apple, the only things not protected with encryption through iCloud is Mail (because email clients already provide their own security) and iTunes in the Cloud, since music does not contain any personal information.

KEYCHAIN

Have you logged onto a website for the first time in ages and forgot what kind of password you used? This happens to everyone; some websites require special characters or phrases, while others require small 8-character passwords. iCloud comes with a highly encrypted feature called Keychain that allows you to store passwords and login information in one place. Any of your Apple devices synced with the same iCloud account will be able to load the data from Keychain without any additional steps.

To activate and start using Keychain, simply click on Settings > iCloud and toggle Keychain on, then follow the prompts. After you've added accounts and passwords to Keychain, your Safari browser will automatically fill in fields while you remain logged into iCloud. If you are ready to checkout after doing some online shopping, for example, the credit card information will automatically pre-fill so you don't have to enter any sensitive information at all.

BATTERY TIPS

The iPhone Pro promises better battery life—the longest ever, in fact. But let's face it, no matter how great the battery is, you probably would love to have just a little bit more life in your charge.

Disable Notifications

My mom told me her battery didn't seem to be lasting very long. I looked at her phone and could not believe how many notifications were activated. She knows absolutely nothing about stocks, nor does she have any desire to learn, and yet she had stock tickers going. You might want notifications on something like Facebook, but there are probably dozens of notifications running in the background that you don't even know about, nor do you even need to. Getting rid of them is easy; go to Settings, then to Notifications. Anything that shows up as "In Notification Center" is currently active on your phone. To disable them, tap on the app and then switch it to off. They aren't gone for good; anytime you want to turn them back on, just go to the very bottom where it says, "Not In Notification Center" and switch them back on.

Brightness

Turning down the brightness just a shade can do wonders for your phone and might even give your eyes some needed relief. It's easy to do; go to Settings, then to Brightness. Just move the slider to a setting that you feel comfortable with.

Email

I prefer to know when I get email as soon as it comes. By doing this, my phone is constantly refreshing email to see if anything has come in; this drains the battery, but not too terribly. If you are the kind of person who doesn't really care when they get email, then it might be good to just switch it from automatic to manual. That way it only checks email when you tap the Mail button. To switch manual on, go to Settings, then to Mail, Contacts, Calendars, and finally go to Fetch New Data. Now go to the bottom and tap "Manually" (you can always switch it back later).

Location, Location, Lo…Battery Hog

Have you heard of location-based apps? These apps use your location to determine where you are exactly. It's actually a great feature if you are using a map of some sort. So, let's say you are looking for somewhere to eat and you have an app that recommends restaurants, it uses your GPS to determine your location so it can tell what's nearby. That is great for some apps, but it is not so great for others. Anytime you use GPS, it's going to drain your battery, so it's a good idea to see what apps are using it and question if you really want them to. Additionally, you can turn it off completely and switch it on only when needed. To do either, go to Settings, then to Location Services, switch any app you don't want using this service to off (you can always switch it back on later).

Accessorize

Ninety percent of you will probably be completely content with these fixes and happy with your battery life; but if you still want more, consider buying a battery pack. Battery packs do make your phone a bit more bulky (they slide on and attach to the back of your phone), but they also give you several more hours of life. They cost around $70. Additionally, you can get an external battery charger to slip in your purse or briefcase. These packs let you charge any USB device (including iPhones and iPads). External battery chargers cost about the same; the one advantage of a charger versus a pack is it will charge any device that has a USB, not just the iPhone.

The easiest way to save battery life, however, is to go to Settings > Battery and switch on "Low Power Mode." This is not the ideal setting for normal phone use, but if you only have 20% of your battery and need it to last longer, then it's there.

ABOUT THE AUTHOR

Scott La Counte is a librarian and writer. His first book, *Quiet, Please: Dispatches from a Public Librarian* (Da Capo 2008) was the editor's choice for the Chicago Tribune and a Discovery title for the Los Angeles Times; in 2011, he published the YA book The N00b Warriors, which became a #1 Amazon bestseller; his most recent book is *#OrganicJesus: Finding Your Way to an Unprocessed, GMO-Free Christianity* (Kregel 2016).

He has written dozens of best-selling how-to guides on tech products.

You can connect with him at ScottDouglas.org.